The Italian Wine Lover's Bible

Never Let a Wine Snob Make You Feel Small

By Global Wine Marketer and Lecturer

Michael Aloysius O'Reilly

© 2015 Michael Aloysius O'Reilly

All rights reserved. No part of this publication may be reproduced or transmitted in any form or by any means, electronic or mechanical, including photocopying, recording, or any information storage and retrieval system, without permission in writing from the publisher. Any resemblance to events or to persons, living or dead is purely coincidental.

Other Books by Michael Aloysius O'Reilly

The Wine Lover's Bible

Compendium: The Wine Lover's Bible

The California Wine Lover's Bible

The French Wine Lover's Bible

Proud Patrick   a Novel

MORNMOR Publishing
Chapel Hill, NC 27516

ISBN-13: 978-1508934929

Il vino è il latte dei vecchi/ Wine is the Milk of the Old—Italian Proverb

Now don't say you can't swear off drinking; it's easy. I've done it a thousand times—W. C. Fields

Cent Anni!/ May You Live a Hundred Years!— Italian Toast

Introduction

THE ITALIAN WINE LOVER'S BIBLE aims to soothe those humble and skittish wine aficionados who wish a beginning knowledge of Italian wine. The journey can seem daunting but it is not.

Question: How does one get their intellectual arms and taste buds around a land growing 2,000 varietal wines in one million vineyards?

The answer: One wine a night over many, many nights.

The first rule for those on bended knee with a wish to know why they adore the wines of Italy is: Italy is a country of red wines. Much white is made but it is rarely important. My apologies to Pinot Grigio and Trebbiano but you guys are not among the great whites of the world. You are nice like slim teenage girls with minimal bumps who will never morph into curvaceous women.

Today Italy is the greatest volume producer of wine in the world. (From vintage to vintage, France can be number one.) Cheap and dear, outrageous in complex beauties or simple pleasures, the wines of Italy--sixty percent of total annual production--are exported throughout the world.

This book aims to elucidate for ardent emerging oenophiles (from the Greek--literally lovers of wine) the regions responsible for the greatest Italian reds and the producers who year after year display passionate artistry to the grapes of their vineyards.

The international wine world accords Bordeaux Cabernet Sauvignon based wines and Pinot Noir from Burgundy as the highest expression that grapes can attain. I will argue that this is wrong. That this is an opinion foisted on us by the Brits who were the great importers, and subsequently the exporters of what they call 'claret'—the reds of the Bordeaux region--and the reds and whites of Burgundy.

Google and Amazon are shining examples of 'the first in their field will rule the field'. So too did Bordeaux wines seize the high ground in greatness. The five Premier Cru Classé (First Growths) today attain the highest global prices vintage after vintage.

I will argue that several red varietals from several regions share the lofty title: greatest in the world. Cabernet Sauvignon (blended with Petit Verdot, Merlot, Cabernet Franc and Malbec—the classic Bordeaux blend) will forever share the pantheon of great reds. But so too will Sangiovese, Nebbiolo, Corvina and Aglianico of Italy. And Pinot Noir from Burgundy and elsewhere. And Syrah and Grenache. These wines all mature into elegant, brilliant wines. And just what is proof of which is the best? This is the task of oenophiles everywhere: to sort out through tastings of all the various vintages with friends and family.

A wonderful change—that quickly rocked the wine world--began in Tuscany in the early 1970s. The Marchese Piero Antinori blended Cabernet Sauvignon with Sangiovese, the ubiquitous grape of Tuscany. This momentous and daring feat profelled the arc of Tuscan wine into greatness. This happened at about the same time that Napa Valley was shocking wine lovers in the USA. Antinori began to produce Tignanello--80% Sangiovese with 20% Cabernet Sauvignon--and Solaia--80% Cabernet Sauvignon with 20% Sangiovese. Antinori's work marked the ascension of Italian wine from cheap and ubiquitous to great…and ubiquitous.

THE ITALIAN WINE LOVER'S BIBLE starts its story from the early 1970s and explores Italy's path to greatness. The great regions and producers are explored. And so too are the varietals--both those native to Italy and those non-native varietals latterly introduced. And, yes, Italy learned from France and New World winegrowers many modern viticultural techniques and vinification inroads. Italy also began importing 55-gallon French oak barrels for aging.

A star was being born.

I

The History of Wine in Italy

Rome's conquest of France (Gaul) is responsible for the dissemination and introduction of the great varietals now known throughout the globe. Rome first brought cuttings from Greece to what is now the Italian boot. The Greeks had brought cuttings from Mesopotamia. The Greeks too probably brought cuttings directly to the boot. The wine drinkers of the world are the beneficiaries.

There are a few Italian wines dubbed 'Greco' that hail back to Greek origins.

Over more than 2,000 years grape varieties were chosen that best were suited to each microclimate. These varieties changed slowly over the centuries a process both of natural selection and successful experiences by the vineyard owners. Cuttings were brought and planted. If they succeeded they stayed, if not they were not replanted. Historical evolution of grape varietals had nothing to do with science and everything to do with practical necessity. And genetic mutation.

We start this book with the early 1970s when Antinori broke the rules of Tuscany and mark that time as the onset of Italian wine greatness.

II

Vineyard Practices

This Chapter is excerpted, in part, from THE WINE LOVER'S BIBLE, the first book in this series. If the reader has not exposed himself/herself to the first book, this chapter is crucial to understanding not only Italy but vineyards throughout the world.

In the past three or four decades there has been a profound change in wine quality as winemakers turned their energy away from steps taken in the winery and the laboratory to enhance their wines. Instead they have brought intense focus onto vineyard practices. Winemakers are now apt to refer to themselves as "winegrowers" given the newly accepted art and science that the quality of the wine is less impacted by what happens in the winery and more profoundly by what happens in the vineyard. For this we have to thank California, New Zealand and Australia for leading the way. The Old World winemakers have seen the light and followed.

Here follows a road map of vineyard practices, some new, some traditional, that are employed to improve wine quality.

The Scourge of Phylloxera

Late in the 19th Century in France and in the 1980s in California, phylloxera appeared causing immense damage to vineyards.

Phylloxera is a subterranean vineyard pest, an aphid or louse. (As mouse is to mice so louse is to lice.) This pest in the soil infects a vineyard by chewing on certain rootstocks that the louse finds delicious. The vines die in spreading, concentric circles from the original infestation. Some rootstocks, such as North American native varietals, the louse will not chew. The challenge is to use rootstocks that the louse dislikes. Because when the phylloxera louse finds delicious rootstocks, it chews and chews until the vines die.

Phylloxera does not thrive in sandy soils.

France never had a phylloxera problem until some unknown individual carried New World *vitis vinifera* cuttings back to France. The vine cuttings—with random infestations of the louse on accompanying soil from America—brought phylloxera to the French wine industry and nearly wiped it out. This disaster began about 1860.

Steamships crossed the Atlantic at that time at faster speeds than sailing ships offered. Perhaps that is why the lice/aphids were still alive when those cuttings were introduced to French vineyards. (Why would anyone take American cuttings to France? No one knows.)

The louse was first identified as the cause of the blight destroying vineyards in Languedoc in the south of France in the 1860s. Through the end of the 19th Century great swaths of French vineyards were destroyed by phylloxera. French winemakers, newly unemployed, took cuttings of Cabernet Sauvignon, Chardonnay and Sauvignon Blanc to phylloxera-free Romania, Bulgaria, Slovenia, Spain, Croatia, Hungary and Moldova and established those varietals previously unknown in those lands. The soils in those countries did not encourage phylloxera and French vines were thus introduced. To the benefit of those countries to be sure.

How did France recover from this scourge? By planting native (*vitis labrusca* and *vitis riparia*) American rootstocks. And then grafting *vitis vinifera* cuttings onto the rootstocks. Remember that the louse/aphid did not find native American varieties (by definition not *vitis vinifera*) delicious and chose not to chew upon them. Also the louse does not thrive in sandy soils; so many North American, South American and European vineyards were spared the scourge. French nurseries propagated North American rootstocks and those were planted and *vitis vinifera* cuttings were then hand or bench grafted to the native American rootstocks. This was a fifty year process. The subterranean pest was deprived of its feeding grounds in France.

Phylloxera is no longer a problem in France. The North American rootstocks solved the French problem although at great expense. The Anatolia region of Turkey, of all places, became (until the French starved the louse utilizing North American rootstock) the greatest source of table wine for the French people at the end of the 19th Century.

Then in the 1980s California was struck with phylloxera. By using native rootstocks the Americans had bypassed the French disaster. But then with the introduction of a new rootstock in the 1960s that was reputed by its French developers to increase grape quality and quantity things changed for the worse.

The villain was a French-developed hybrid rootstock: AxR1.

As the infestation of phylloxera metastasized, the French pointed fingers at the University of California at Davis saying: "We told you so. We told you not to plant AxR1. Because that AxR1 is not phylloxera resistant!" The academics at Davis denied they ever got the e-mail. Perhaps because there was no e-mail in the 1960s.

In any event, California was forced to rip up tens of thousands of acres of phylloxera-stricken vineyards beginning in the 1980s. Once the vines were uprooted the Californians used extensive fumigation to kill off the infestation still in the soil. New plantings replaced the AxR1 rootstock with rootstock not delicious to the aphids/lice. The nurseries propagating the rootstock made a lot of money that this disaster occasioned. The extraordinary expense of tearing out (literally extirpating) and then replanting vineyards brought about many distress sales of California vineyards.

All is now well in France, California and around the world. For the present anyways. Growing grapes is a dicey economic risk.

Like all crops grape vines are subject to too much moisture or drought, extreme cold, extreme heat and....lice. The payoff is that no agricultural product obtains anywhere near the prices that wine grapes bring in the market place.

Traditional Head Pruning

Traditional head pruning each Spring involves snipping off the prior vintage's branches. This leaves a Medusa-like black gnarled stumps. The coming vintage will grow from these stumpy branches year after year. For the field workers, this is back breaking work in that the vines are rarely higher than three feet.

The practice is disappearing. Head pruning produced great wines over the centuries but as we will see vineyard practices have eclipsed tradition bringing grape yields and grape quality to new heights.

Vine Life

The typical life of a vine is 25 years. Why not let the vines produce forever? Because s vines age grape yields shrink. The berries get smaller so that the ratio of juice to skin is not favorable. This diminishing yield is not to be ignored. As yields decline to a ton and a half per acre at harvest, or even lower, extirpating the old vines and replanting is taken up. The young vines will take up two or three vintages without much yield. However the new plantings will commonly feature advances in regard to trellis choices, vine spacing and rootstock selection.

There are hundred year old vines. Not many but I have seen such in California mostly planted to Zinfandel producing such extraordinary wine that the vineyard owner continues to harvest each year. This is rare.

Vine Density

How many vines per acre are optimal? Vines are planted in rows. In the row, how close or far should the next vine be?

Between the rows, how close should the next row be? How many vines per acre will produce quality?

Traditional planting in France has been 1 meter by 1 meter (approximately 3' x 3') meaning up to 4,380 vines per acre. Traditional planting in California had been 5' x 7' feet or 1,240 vines per acre. (Europeans use hectares as a measurement of land rather than acres. A hectare is approximately 2.5 acres. For simplicity, I have set forth all comparisons in acres.)

France was planting much more tightly but just how densely could a California vineyard be planted before wine quality suffered? Obviously the French had been doing a pretty good job. But California was doing pretty well too. Did denser plantings increase or decrease wine quality? Was dense planting worth the investment? What was optimal and why was there such a shocking difference in vine spacing in France and California? One reason was economic. France traditionally used manual labor to prune branches and pick the grapes of their 'head trained' vines, vines that looked like a Medusa's head but adorned with branches instead of snakes. Intense vineyard management during the growing season adds enormously to the final cost of grapes.

From the days when the first Missions were established, California used carts pulled by a horse, donkey or mule to harvest the grapes. The workers walking behind the cart, snipped the clusters and tossed them into the cart. Or the workers filled manageable one-man hoppers and walked them to a central cart. After World War II, mechanical harvesters were introduced to bring in the grapes. This was certainly more economical than manual labor but oftentimes this was a violent method of harvesting. The vine stumps were shaken until the clusters fell onto conveyer belts. In this manner a fraction of the grapes was crushed inadvertently and juice collected at the bottom of the field cart or hopper. This juice was immediately subject to oxidation; not a good idea for freshness.

California was thusly mechanized and therefore could show cost savings through mechanical harvesting. This is not surprising in that California wine prior to the 1960s was largely an industrial affair. Quality was not sought as much as quantity and success was measured by the bottom line. Until the 1960s half of California's wine was fortified in the winery with brandy to pack more of a punch. There are zero fortified wines now coming out of Napa Valley today. (This is not entirely true as a few make Port-like dessert wines.)

When the Californians figured out that their wine spacing was purely industrial, i.e. more conducive to getting a donkey and a cart comfortably between the rows, they began to follow the French lead in regard to dense vine spacing. From the early 1980s all sorts of experiments were made. Many of the quality vineyards--those that could command high prices for grapes and wine--as they were replanted after the phylloxera scourge of the 1980s (see phylloxera above) moved to dense spacing.

An extraordinary quality surge followed. Rather than harvesting 4-6 tons per acre with the 5' x'7 spacing it was discovered that with the greater densities many vineyards in the Napa Valley were able to increase production and able to harvest 8 and even 10 tons per acre! And increase grape quality at the same time! The acreage was expensive to plant and the vines had to be pruned and picked by hand as mechanical harvesting went out the door but wine quality made a great leap forward. With the dense plantings, berries got smaller meaning there was less juice and more skin which added flavor. Do remember that red wine quality is largely determined by the skin color at harvest. Deeper color makes for better quality. Smaller berries make for more intense wines.

Later narrow mechanical harvesters were introduced by Japanese manufacturers; these behemoths did not operate between vine rows but actually straddled a row. So goes the constant search for efficiency. And profit. The wineries nurture the romance of wine in their marketing. But woe to the winery that does not respect the bottom line. Like any business.

The dense head pruned vines in traditional French vineyards have slowly been replanted with trellis systems for optimal sun, humidity control and cluster quality. And to avoid manual labor.

Understanding vne spacing is just one of the advancements toward our arriving at The Golden Age of Wine. It's never been better.

Trellising

Traditional head pruning is still in practice in many vineyards. Many California vineyards have morphed to equally dense plantings aping French density but the vines are trellised, i.e. the branches are trained to grow along wires giving each cluster an equal chance to get sunlight. This has led to higher yields and grapes that mature simultaneously. A vineyard with modern trellising will likely only have to be picked only once.

Next time you are around vineyards, look for bi-lateral cordon pruning. This trellising aims for exposing clusters to sun (but not too much), increasing grape yields, and facilitating grape harvesting. There can be a danger with this training in vineyards subject to strong winds like both Northern and Southern Rhône wines which are subject to the Mistral.

Also see if you can pick out single cordon trellising and differentiate the two. Should be obvious. Look for lyre training. The vines are trained to look like lyres!

Vine Pruning

Late winter, before the vines wake up to the new season, the old producing branches are cut back to allow for new growth. (See head pruning above.) This pruning period begins in February and lasts about six weeks.

Vine tipping during the growing season involves pruning the excess growth of branches with leaves that detract from the energy the vine is imparting to growing grape sugars. Unproductive leaves and branches are a negative but this viticultural practice is mainly limited to high value vineyards.

Bud Break

In Spring the first green shoots or buds show themselves. The growing season moves next to "shatter" when the primitive clusters appear; soon followed by tiny very acidic clusters of nuggets that will, through photosynthesis, grow into ripe sweet grapes. Table grapes in your supermarket may be 11-14 Brix. (Brix is a measurement of sugar solids.) Sweet but tart also. Grapes for wine are harvested far sweeter. Grapes destined to be wine will have sugars that measure between 17-25 Brix depending on what the microclimate will allow and the aims of the winemaker.

Microclimate: Rain, Dirt and Sunshine

A microclimate is an area conducive to winegrowing. It's a complex equation, a sum of several characteristics. There is sufficient but not too much rainfall both during the growing season and in the winter. Soils are involved: clay can be a negative because it will retain moisture and the vine will have too much vigor devoted to growing leaves. Well drained rock and/or volcanic soils are desirable so that the vine will stress itself reaching deep for moisture. Tap roots in Napa Valley can descend twelve feet or more.

A pregnant woman's body will send nutrients first and foremost to the fetus and then to herself. The same is true of the vine: nutrition to the grape cluster first and foremost and only secondarily to the leafy canopy shielding the grapes from sun. A viticulturalist described this to me wonderfully: The ultimate purpose of a vine is to give off grapes which give up their seeds and propagate new vines.

A German winemaker in the Nahe can wish for or aim for 24 Brix but his grapes will never get there. The growing season is simply not hot enough in Germany. Mainz, along the Rhine River, experiences an average August 24 hour temperature of 60.8°F, 1.5" of rain and 6.7 hours of sunshine including an average of ten days with cloudy weather.

The average temperature over 24 hours in Burgundy in August is 65.7°F. Warmer than Germany to be sure. And able, therefore, to produce great red wines which is really not possible in

Germany. Average August rainfall is 2.1" in Burgundy with but 6 hours of sunshine daily.

In Napa Valley average August 24-hour temperatures range from 68°F in the southerly City of Napa with 10 hours of sunshine and higher at the north end of the valley in Calistoga at 72°F. Twelve degrees Fahrenheit warmer than in the Nahe! Rainfall in August in Napa is almost non-existent at .1" for the month. Soils on the hillsides are volcanic, thin and well drained. Vines seek moisture on the benches, the bottom of the hillsides, and this stresses the vines producing the finest grapes. Burgundy's limestone slopes reflect this same phenomenon: flat land at the bottom of the slopes produces less quality than the stressed vines on the slopes higher up. Napa's clays have washed down toward the Napa River over the centuries. Those soils retain more moisture.

These readings tell the story!

Therefore, dear reader, before you buy your first vineyard at $200,000 or more per acre do your due diligence and determine what you can expect in heat, rainfall, dirt and sunshine. Because your grapes turned to wine will reflect the microclimate's dirt, heat, sunshine and rainfall.

Period.

We see clearly Napa Valley as a true representative of New World wines with warm temperatures, low rainfall and lots of sun.

Burgundy's greatest vintages are those with minimal rainfall during the growing season and harvest, higher than average temperature and much sunshine. The same is true of Germany. Great blow-your-horn vintages may occur only three times in any given decade in Germany and France. The weather is a roll of the dice.

But don't pity Germany with its clouds, rain and cool temperatures. German winemakers may actually be the best in the world as they eke out wines of great finesse in microclimates that are to say the least challenging.

Frost

Frost danger exists during the Spring for the young shoots following bud break and prior to the formation of clusters (shatter). Temperatures below freezing during this time can have disastrous consequences for the vintage.

Both for orange groves and vineyards, growers had for a long time used petroleum smudge pots on the perimeter of the crop. This elevated ambient temperature but was labor intensive and added to pollution.

Protection can be achieved in a counterintuitive manner: by spraying the vines with water. As the ambient temperature descends below freezing, a thin blanket of ice forms on the buds which actually keeps the young buds warm! Inside the ice blanket, the buds do not lose heat. The ice guarantees against this. Go figure!

Photosynthesis

Remember photosynthesis from High School Biology? The following experiment was published by Jan Baptisa van Helmont in 1648: "...I took an earthenware vessel, placed in it 200 pounds of soil dried in an oven, soaked this with rainwater, and planted in it a willow branch weighing 5 pounds. At the end of five years, the tree that had grown from it weighed 169 pounds and about 3 ounces. Now, the earthenware vessel was always moistened (when necessary) only with rainwater or distilled water, and it was large enough and embedded in the ground, and, lest dust flying be mixed with the soil, an iron plate coated with tin and pierced by many holes covered the rim of the vessel. I did not compute the weight of the fallen leaves of the four autumns. Finally I dried the soil in the vessel again, and the same 200 pounds were found, less about 2 ounces. Therefore 169 pounds of wood, bark, and root had arisen from water only." Most of the weight gain of the tree described in the above experiment came from sunlight, carbon dioxide and water. The equation for photosynthesis shows that these compounds are used to produce glucose, a form of sugar.

During July and August grape clusters add sugars. This reduces the ratio of acidity to sweetness. Rain and cool weather bring the dangers of mold and low sugar levels. Too much heat—temperatures over 100°F--and the vines will shut down and there is also a danger of "burn" in the clusters—simply too hot and bright a sun.

Canopy Management

For clusters to get enough but not too much sun, modern viticulture--for wines of great quality and price—has taken to lopping off excessive leaf foliage. (See above: vine tipping.) The aim here to let the vigor of the vine go to the grape clusters and not to those leaves and branches that do not bear grape clusters. Some quality wineries will have the vineyard workers lop off excess foliage two and even three times during the growing season. Too much sun and the grapes will burn, get an undesirable sun tan. Too much foliage means that the vine is working too hard at producing leaves not sweet grapes. The quality regions are more likely to engage in this practice as a crew passing through the vines, whether to lop off excess foliage or dropping fruit to the ground to encourage more color for the remaining clusters, is expensive. Inexpensive table wines do not receive this sort of attention.

Sun Orientation

In the northern hemisphere the sun rises in the southeast and warms our days while on the way to sunset in the southwest. Scientific inquiry has been intense the past several decades aimed at planting vines that optimize exposure to sun. Should one plant vine rows north to south? East to west? These decisions will impact the vineyard and the vine spacing. Also affected will be the heat created on the vineyard floor during the day. And the exposure of the grape clusters to the sun. Not too much, not too little. And wind must be considered. High windy areas will encourage foliage above the grape clusters.

Natural Air Conditioning and Humidity

High moisture environments need a natural 'air conditioning' to avoid bunch rot. (In the absence of cooling air, sulfuring is employed to manage rot. But any residual sulfur on harvested grapes will retard wine expressiveness.) Each microclimate is a study in itself. Vineyards near rivers, lakes and coastal regions may experience high humidity. This requires the planting of vines to allow for maximum ventilation. From where do the winds blow in this region? Vineyards are planted so that the wind will travel through the vines rows and reduce humidity minimizing the danger and bunch rot. This is a farming technique to take advantage of the particularities of the microclimate.

Dropping Good Fruit

A bountiful harvest can mean less than optimum wines. The vines will have so many clusters to ripen they will fail to produce optimum sugars. The reverse is true; a small harvest can mean a great harvest. Grape size means juice in ratio to skin. There it is! Small berries with great color will make the best red wine.

And then there are huge crops such as California experienced in 1974; perhaps the vintage of the century in terms of great, long-lived wines of extraordinary color and fruit all happening in a huge harvest.

In September and early October, as the winemaker and the viticulturist put their heads together, they want to not only optimize grape sugars but also to await optimum skin color. And sugars that will be balanced with the grapes' acidity. They may choose to have the workers drop fruit onto the ground so that the final oomph in the growing season is dedicated to not volume but to skin color. They are inducing the vines to lend their vigor to the remaining clusters. This is not the industrial model of vineyard management. However the results can be spectacular. Oh do the wines taste good! Only the best of the fine wine guys will do this. Let us praise winemakers who drop good fruit on the ground in order to make an even greater wine from those clusters not dropped.

Cluster Rot, Berry Rot

Mechanical harvesters—not being intelligent--will harvest fruit that has mold. Mold or rot (not noble rot which we'll see further on) is going to produce off flavors. In the high value hand-picked vineyards, workers pass over bad bunches. Or on sorting tables after the crop is brought in, they separate individual moldy berries from the cluster while allowing healthy berries and clusters to advance to the stemmer-crusher.

Stuff happens. Pick around it.

Desire to know more of modern viticulture? Let me point you to the man who wrote the book(s) on viticulture: Dr. Richard E. Smart of New Zealand. From his website, I now pass on many of his published contributions to understanding soil, trellising, canopy management, leaf tipping, sun exposure, and humidity management in vine rows. Smart may be the key New World contributor to 20th Century knowledge of grape growing. And the work continues.

1.SMART, R.E. & Coombe, B.G., 1983. Water relations of grapevines. Additional woody crop plants. In: Water Deficiencies and Plant Growth. T.T. KOZLOWSKI (ed), Academic Press, N.Y. VII, pp. 138-188.

2.SMART, R.E., CLARKE, A.D. & Wheeler, S.J., 1986. Grapevines. In: CLARKE, C.J., G.S. SMITH, I.S. CORNFORTH & M. PRASAD (eds.) Fertiliser recommendations for horticultural crops. New Zealand MAF Occasional Publication.

3.DRY, P.R. & SMART,R.E., 1988. Chapter 2. The Grapegrowing Regions of Australia. In: COOMBE, B. & P. DRY (eds.) Viticulture. Vol 1. Resources in Australia. Winetitles, Adelaide. pp. 37-60.

4.DRY, P.R. & SMART, R.E., 1988. Chapter 10. Vineyard Site Selection. In: COOMBE, B. & P. DRY (eds.) Viticulture. Vol.1. Resources in Australia. Winetitles, Adelaide. pp. 190-204.

5.SMART, R.E., Thornton, R.J., Rodriguez, S.B. & Young, J.E. 1988.. (Eds) Proc. of the Second International Symposium for Cool Climate Viticulture and Oenology, Auckland, N.Z. N.Z. Soc. for Viticulture and Oenology. 365pp.

6.Kliewer, W.M. & SMART, R.E. 1989. Canopy manipulation for optimizing vine microclimate, crop yield and composition of grapes. In: WRIGHT, C.J. (ed.) Manipulation of fruiting. Butterworths, London. pp. 275-292.

7.SMART, R. & Robinson, M. 1991. Sunlight Into Wine. A handbook for winegrape canopy management. Winetitles, Adelaide. 88 pp.

8.SMART, R.E., 1992. Chapter 5. Canopy management. In: COOMBE, B & P. DRY (eds.) Viticulture, Vol.2. Practices. Winetitles, Adelaide. pp. 85-103.

9.Robinson, J. (Ed). The Oxford Companion to Wine. Oxford University Press, Oxford, 1994. 1088 pp (R. Smart was the Viticulture Editor, responsible for about 12% of all entries,the third largest contributor. His major contributions are marked by the initials R.E.S.).

10.Robinson, J. (Ed). The Oxford Companion to Wine. Oxford University Press, Oxford, 1999. 818 pp (R. Smart was the Viticulture Editor. His major contributions are marked by the initials R.E.S.).

11.Robinson, J. (Ed). The Oxford Companion to Wine. Oxford University Press, Oxford, 2006. 813 pp (R. Smart was the Viticulture Editor. His major contributions are marked by the initials R.E.S.).

12.SMART, R.E. & GILBY, C., 2004. Viticulture. In: STEVENSON, T, & KINDERSLEY, D., Wine Report 2004, Doring Kindersley Ltd, London, pp. 369-376.

13.SMART, R.E. & GILBY, C., 2005. Viticulture. In: STEVENSON, T, & KINDERSLEY, D., Wine Report 2005, Doring Kindersley Ltd, London

14.SMART, R.E. & GILBY, C., 2006. Viticulture. In: STEVENSON, T, & KINDERSLEY, D., Wine Report 2006, Doring Kindersley Ltd, London

15.SMART, R.E. & GILBY, C., 2007. Viticulture. In: STEVENSON, T, & KINDERSLEY, D., Wine Report 2007, Doring Kindersley Ltd, London, pp. 380-386.

THESES

1.SMART, R.E., 1971. Aspects of light use by vineyards. M.Sc. Hons. Thesis, Macquarie University, Eastwood, NSW, Australia. 137 pp.

2.SMART, R.E., 1976. Implications of the radiation microclimate for productivity of vineyards. Ph.D. Thesis, Cornell University, Ithaca, NY, USA. 174 pp.

3.SMART, R.E., 1995, The effects of manipulating grapevine vigour and canopy microclimate on yield, grape composition and wine quality. D.Sc. (Agrc) Thesis, Universtiy of Stellenbosch, South Africa. 339 pp.

SCIENTIFIC PAPERS IN NON PEER REVIEWED SCIENTIFIC

JOURNALS AND CONFERENCE/SEMINAR PROCEEDINGS

1.SMART, R.E., 1968. A new root observation chamber. Proc. Aust. Fruit Res. Conference, Mildura, Australia. pp. 137-138.

2.SMART, R.E., 1968. A model of the photosynthetically active radiation environment of a vineyard. Proc. Aust. Fruit Res. Conference, Mildura, Australia. pp. 11-12.

3.SMART, R.E., 1969. Irrigation, grape yield and wine quality. (Abstract only) 41st ANZAAS Conference. Adelaide.

4.SMART, R.E., 1970. Solar radiation interception as a guide to the design of horticultural plantings. (Abstract only) Proc. of the XVIII International Horticultural Congress, Tel Aviv, Israel.

5.SMART, R.E., 1970. Photosynthesis of vine canopies. (Abstract only) Proc. of the XVIII International Horticultural Congress, Tel Aviv, Israel.

6.SMART, R., 1971. Light use in grape production. Proc. Viticultural Symposium, Griffith, Australia. pp. 1-12.

7.SMART, R., 1971. Grapes, wine and water. Proc. Griffith Vintage Festival Symposium. Griffith, Australia. pp. 31-46.

8.SMART, R.E., 1973. Water needs of wine grapes. Proc. of the 2nd Aust. Wine Industry Technical Conference, Tanunda, Australia. Aust. Wine Res. Institute. pp. 7-10.

9.Shaulis, N.J., SMART, R.E., 1974. Grapevine canopies: management, microclimate, and yield responses. Proc. XIX International Horticultural Congress. Warsaw, Poland. 3, 255-265.

10.SMART, R.E.. & Dry, P.R., (eds.) 1976. Grapevine pruning. Do we need to mechanise? Proceedings of a Workshop. Roseworthy, Australia. Roseworthy Agricultural College. 28 pp.

11.SMART, R.E., Dry, P.R. & Bruer, D.R.G., 1977. Field temperatures of grape berries and implications for fruit composition. Proc. OIV

International Symposium on The Quality of the Vintage. Cape Town, South Africa.

12. SMART, R.E.. 1977. Climate and grapegrowing in Australia. Proc. of the 3rd Aust. Wine Industry Technical Conference, Albury, Australia. Aust. Wine res. Institute. pp 12-18.

13. SMART, R.E.. & Kyloh, S.R., (eds.) 1979. Mechanical pruning of grapevines. Proceedings of a Workshop. Roseworthy, Australia. Roseworthy Agricultural College and the Australian Wine Board. 99 pp.

14. SMART, R.E. & Dry, P.R. (eds.) 1979. Vineyard site selection for quality winegrape production. Roseworthy, Australia. Roseworthy Agricultural College. 153 pp.

15. SMART, R.E. & KYLOH, S.R., (eds.) 1980. Mechanical pruning of grapevines. Proceedings of a Workshop. Roseworthy, Australia. Roseworthy Agricultural College and the Australian Wine Board. 54 pp.

16. SMART, R.E., Robinson, J.B. & Due, G.R., 1981. Manipulation of wine quality within the vineyard. Proc. seminar, Grape quality assessment from vineyard to juice preparation. Aust. Soc. of Viticulture and Oenology. Melbourne, Australia. pp. 19-27.

17. SMART, R.E., 1982. Vine manipulation to improve wine grape quality. Proc. University of California, Davis, Grape and Wine Centennial Symposium. Davis, California. University of California. pp. 362-375.

18. SMART, R.E., Carbonneau, A. & De Loth, C., 1982. Application a l'etude synthetique des principaux facteurs de milieu expliquant la hierarchie des crus. Exemple de la qualite du vin de Cabernet Sauvignon dans l'appellation 'Graves de Bordeaux'. Vignes et vins numero special Sept. 1982. Proc. Seminaire Agromeleorologie et Vigne, 1981. 87-94.

19. Clarke, A. & SMART, R.E., 1982. MAF tentative rootstock recommendations - June, 1982. Proc. MAF Phylloxera Seminar, Gisborne, N.Z. 68 pp.

20.SMART, R.E., 1982. Choosing the correct material for grafting. MAF Phylloxera Seminar, Gisborne, N.Z. 68 pp.

21.King, P.D., SMART, R.E. & Stephens, P.R., 1982. 1982 Phylloxera survey results. MAF Phylloxera Seminar, Gisborne, N.Z. 10 pp.

22.SMART, R.E., 1983. Vineyard canopies of the future. Proc. Centenary Grape and Wine Symposium. Roseworthy Agricultural College, SA, Australia. pp. 1-28.

23.Gould, B. & SMART, R.E., 1983. Grapevine imports into New Zealand - past, present and future. Proc. Vintage '83 Seminar, Te Kauwhata, N.Z. Te Kauwhata Oenological and Viticultural Bulletin 36, 9 pp.

24.SMART, R.E., 1983. Improving wine quality in the vineyard. I. Proc. of Vintage '83 Seminar. Te Kauwhata Oenological and Viticultural Bulletin 36, 14 pp.

25.SMART, R.E., 1984. Canopy microclimates and effects on wine quality. Proc. of the 5th Australian Wine Industry Technical Conference, Perth, WA, Australia. Aust. Wine Research Institute. pp. 113-132.

26.SMART, R.E., 1984. Improving wine quality in the vineyard II. Proc. of Vintage '84 Seminar. Te Kauwhata, N.Z. Te Kauwhata Oenological and Viticultural Bulletin 43, 24pp.

27.SMART, R.E., 1984. Some aspects of climate, canopy microclimate, vine physiology and wine quality. Proc. International Symposium on Cool Climate Viticulture and Enology, Eugene, U.S.A. Oregon State University. pp. 1-19.

28.SMART, R.E. & King, P.D., 1984. Grapevine phylloxera in New Zealand. Proc. of the 5th Australian Wine Industry Technical Conference, Perth, Australia. Aust. Wine Research Institute. pp. 203-214.

29.SMART, R.E., 1985. (Ed). Grape quality and grape pricing. Proc. of Inaugural Seminar. Grape quality, grape pricing. Gisborne, N.Z., Oct.

1985. N.Z. Soc. for Viticulture and Oenology. 125pp.

30. SMART, R.E., 1985. Measurement of yield and grape quality in the field. Proc. of Inaugural Seminar. Grape quality, grape pricing. Gisborne, N.Z. N.Z. Soc. for Viticulture and Oenology. pp. 14-39.

31. SMART, R.E., 1985. Yield and quality responses to new trellis systems with Gewurztraminer. Vintage '85 Seminar. Te Kauwhata Oenological and Viticultural Bulletin 46, 10-31.

32. Oldman, J.W., Judd, M.J., McAneney, K.J. & SMART, R.E., 1985. Canopy microclimate effects on bunch rot. Proc. of Vintage '85 Seminar. Te Kauwhata Research Station Oenological and Viticultural Bulletin 46, 55-63.

33. SMART, R.E., Smith, Stephen M., Smith, G.S., 1985. Nitrate reductase - a key enzyme affecting wine grape quality? (Abstract only) Proc. of the New Zealand Soc. of Horticultural Science Conference.

34. Jackson, D. & SMART, R.E., 1985. Yield, quality and light use by grapes. Proc. Pacific Northwest Grape Shortcourse, Pasco, WA, U.S.A. Washington State University. pp. 9-23.

35. SMART, R.E., (Ed) 1986. Improving wine quality in the vineyard. Proc. of Seminar, Auckland, N.Z. N.Z. Soc. for Viticulture and Oenology. 100 pp.

36. SMART, R.E. & Smith, Stephen M., 1986. Environmental and plant factors affecting grapevine photosynthesis. Proc. of the International Workshop on Regulation of Photosynthesis in Fruit Crops. Davis, California. pp. 51-58.

37. SMART, R.E. and Smith, S.M., 1986. New Zealand experiences with vineyard manipulations. Proc. of Seminar, Auckland, N.Z. N.Z. Soc. for Viticulture and Oenology. pp. 82-90.

38. SMART, R.E., & Young, J. (eds.) 1986. Proc. of the Winter Pruning Field Day. Te Kauwhata and Gisborne, N.Z. Te Kauwhata Research Station Oenological and Viticultural Bulletin 48, 43 pp.

39.SMART, R.E., 1986. Vine improvement in New Zealand with implications for Oregon. Lecture delivered at and published by Oregon State University. August 22, 1986.

40.SMART, R.E., 1986. Vine improvement research in N.Z. Proc. Vintage '86 Seminar, Napier. Te Kauwhata Oenological and Viticultural Bulletin 47, 24-43.

41.Wood, P.N. & SMART, R.E., 1986. Mueller Thurgau responses to different bud numbers. Proc. Winter Pruning Field Day. Te Kauwhata Oenological and Viticultural Bulletin 48, 15-21.

42.SMART, R.E., 1986. Pruning and training systems. Proc. Winter Pruning Field Day. Te Kauwhata Oenological and Viticultural Bulletin 48, 27-37.

43.SMART, R.E., 1987. Canopy management to improve yield, fruit composition and vineyard mechanisation - a review. Proc. 6th Australian Wine Industry Technical Conference, Adelaide, Australia. Aust. Wine Res. Institute. pp. 205-211.

44.Smith, S.M. & SMART, R.E., 1987. Plant factors affecting grapevine photosynthesis in the field. Proc. Vintage '87 Seminar, Gisborne, N.Z. Te Kauwhata Research Station Oenological and Viticultural Bulletin 51, 19-30.

45.Snaddon, K. & SMART, R.E., 1987. Vineyard responses to grassing down. Proc. Vintage '87 Seminar, Gisborne, N.Z. Te Kauwhata Research Station Oenological and Viticultural Bulletin 51, 31-38.

46.SMART, R.E. & CLARKE, A.D., 1987. Can New Zealand produce bulk winegrapes competitively? Proc. Vintage '87 Seminar, Gisborne, N.Z. Te Kauwhata Research Station Oenological and Viticultural Bulletin 51, 73-84.

47.Eschenbruch, R., SMART, R., Fisher, B. & Whittles, J., 1987. Influence of yield manipulations on the terpene content of juices and wines of Mueller Thurgau. Proc. Sixth Australian Wine Industry

Technical Conference, Adelaide, Australia. Aust. Wine Res. Institute. pp. 89-93.

48. SMART, R.E., 1987. The light quality environment of vineyards. Proc. of Third OIV International Symposium on Vine Physiology, Bordeaux, France, June, 1986. pp. 370-373.

49. SMART, R.E., DRY, P.R. & Loffler, L., 1987. Critical relations of shoot spacing in vineyards. Proc. of Third OIV International Symposium on Vine Physiology, Bordeaux, France, pp. 374-377.

50. SMART, R.E., 1987. Influencia de la luz en la compasicion y la calidad de la uva. Proc. Seminar Uva de Mesa de Exportacion, Santiago, Chile. Catholic University of Chile: 45-58.

51. SMART, R.E. CLARKE, A.D. & Whittles, J, 1987. La industria de uva de mesa en Nueva Zelandia. Proc. Seminar Uva de Mesa de Exportacion, Santiago, Chile. Catholic University of Chile. pp. 203-216.

52. SMART, R.E., Kingston, C.M. & van Epenhuijsen, C.W., 1987. Manejo de la canopia (follaje) para obtener rendimiento y calidad. Proc. Seminar Uva de Mesa de Exportacion, Santiago, Chile. Catholic University of Chile. pp. 229-252.

53. SMART, R.E., & SMITH, S.M., 1988. Canopy management: identifying the problems and practical solutions. Proc. Second International Cool Climate Viticulture and Oenology Symposium, Auckland, N.Z. N.Z. Soc. for Viticulture and Oenology. pp. 109-115.

54. SMART, R.E., 1988. Grape quality and grape pricing - a somewhat philosophical view. Proc. Second International Cool Climate Viticulture and Oenology Symposium, Auckland, N.Z. N.Z. Soc. for Viticulture and Oenology. pp. 191-192.

55. Smith, S., Codrington, I.C., Robertson, M., & SMART, R.E. 1988. Viticultural and oenological implications of leaf removal for New Zealand vineyards. Proc. Second International Cool Climate Viticulture and Oenology Symposium, Auckland, N.Z. pp. 127-133.

Daunting isn't it?

Such studies are the meat and potatoes of the viticulturalists, winemakers and winery owners of our time. To compete economically and artistically such study is mandatory. I expect that few of my readers will ever have the time or the inclination to take up the intense, detailed work of such viticulturalists as Richard Smart.

Then again there are moments that launch careers.

Wine as a hobby is like chess or bridge. You can spend your life at wine, chess or bridge and infinite complexities will keep popping up. After many years of studying wine, you may find that you have hardly scratched the surface. The grand payoff is intellectual knowledge combined with sensory tasting. And, over time, your experience with wine is guaranteed to get richer.

Harvesting at Night

Quality vineyards are harvested beginning as early as 4 a.m. Overnight the water content of the sleeping grapes is lower. Therefore picking while still dark in the early morning hours before the heat of the day yields a more concentrated grape.

Oh Delicious Rot!

Some rotten berries are delicious!

It's called noble rot. The Latin classification is *botrytis cinerea*. In France it is called *Pourriture Noble*. In Germany, the mold is called *Edelfäule* and the wine is labeled *Trockenbeerenauslese* (literally late picked berries). In Italy the mold is *muffa nobile*. In Hungary, *aszúsodás*.

This rot is responsible for some of the world's most delicious and expensive wines. The bacillus attacks grapes after the normal growing season. Like all molds this one prefers clouds to sun and humidity to dryness. The mold feeds itself with a skinny "sucker" that pierces the grape skin and desiccates it, i.e. moisture is extracted causing the sugars to concentrate and rise. Remember that these grapes are not picked until November and the sugars have kept on elevating. A hot November with abundant sunshine will inhibit the growth of the mold. It's a crap shoot and a waiting game. Happy is he who gets his rotten clusters! With wet cool weather and cloudy weather the mold will take hold and the grapes will bear a hazy brown fuzz and the winemaker will finally pick the grapes. He will kill the years and end fermentation--probably by chilling the must—before all the sugars are exhausted by the yeasts. And the result? A dessert wine of 6-12% residual sugar. Sweet like Port but dependent upon the style the winemaker is seeking. And from the rot on the grape skins, a rich honeyed character has developed in the wine. These wines are capable of extended aging.

Alice Nightingale and Winemaker Myron Nightingale, long a fixture at Beringer in the Napa Valley, actually propagated an infection of noble rot in the basement of their home in the early 1970s. They sprayed late harvest Semillon and Sauvignon Blanc with spores of *botrytis cinerea* and produced perhaps the first commercially available—and artificially inoculated--noble rot wine in California.

The sugar and acid in these wines can see them age gracefully and with increasing intensity for one hundred years or more. While aging, the wines turn from deep gold to a brownish red in their later years.

Ice wine (*Eiswein*) from Germany can be yet another rare dessert wine with grapes not picked till frozen in the vineyard, probably after snow has fallen. This treat is very rare. Very expensive too. Rarely, the Finger Lakes in New York produce ice wine from Riesling and also in the Niagara area in the province of Ontario above Niagara Falls. When you find one grab it, age it and pour same for your best friends. They will go crazy with this treat.

Late Harvest wines are not to be confused with noble rot affected grapes. Harvesting grapes after the normal season can produce concentrations of sweetness and honeyed character so wonderful you can skip the ice cream. (Or try it on vanilla ice cream!) Muscat (or Moscato) may be the most available varietal in these late harvest dessert wines. You won't be able to tell the sugar level from the label. Some will have a tinge of sweetness and others rise to be sugary confections.

Andy Quady of California has for decades made Muscat late harvest wines of seriously unctuous beauty. Find a brand you like and thrill your friends. Accomplished wine lovers and neophytes all love dessert wine. Beginners on the road to loving wine will be dazzled by slight sweetness. The American craze for White Zinfandel (which is actually a faint Rosé made from red Zinfandel grapes) is a sign of wine lovers entering the nursery school of wine tasting. They will most likely progress next to light whites like Pinot Grigio and Riesling, then on to big whites like Sauvignon Blanc and Chardonnay, then to delicate reds like Pinot Noir, and onward and upward to mighty reds such as Cabernet Sauvignon, Nebbiolo, Malbec, Zinfandel and Syrah. The payoff and pinnacle for many wine lovers is when they arrive at a love of aged vintage Port. Notice that novices start with off-dry or slightly sweet wine and climb the ladder to the heaven of great Port wine. This is the great journey every wine lover is embarked upon.

Irrigation

Irrigation is used in dry high yield vineyards to increase production. This is necessary to keep the vines producing. In very hot weather—in excess of 100°F—vines will shut down and photosynthesis will stop. There the vines will sit waiting for the heat spell to end. Grape clusters can burn and dramatically affect the harvest in extreme heat.

Most irrigation is drip irrigation for the sake of water conservation. In California the management of water resources has become critical. During the winter rains, Napa wineries may irrigate the dormant vines with the aim of improving the water table in preparation for the growing season. This practice works while the Napa River and the reservoirs are full—or overfull with the excess dumping into San Francisco Bay.

A danger posed by sprayed irrigation during the growing season is the possible propagation of mold. With lots of sun this is not a problem; the molds cannot thrive. Irrigation can be used as a boost to the economics of a winery. More grapes and more wine equals more sales. (Then again stressed vines throw their vigor toward grape sugar.)

Some German vineyards are legally prohibited from the practice of irrigation. Because irrigation is not natural? Probably. There are purists in every profession. Anyway this prohibition can cause much lost sleep by German viticulturalists during a dry growing season as they are forced to sneak into their own vineyards away from the neighbors' spying eyes and under of darkness….irrigate.

If a parched traveler knocked on your door wouldn't you give him a drink of water?

Optimum Harvest

"Ripeness is all." --King Lear

Perhaps the decision as to when to harvest is the most important decision. Will the fruit, after the sugars have been attacked by yeast, balance with the grapes' natural acidity? Winemakers and viticulturalists will be in the vineyard several times a day approaching harvest to measure optimal ripeness.

Question: which is sweeter, an orange or a lemon? A LEMON! There are more sugars and more acid in a lemon than in your favorite orange. High acid will make you pucker but all fruit is different. I've seen winemakers pick a grape, pop it in their clenched teeth and declare 'it's time to pick!' They may also have the workers pick selectively as they go down the vine rows postponing the picking of some immature grapes for another week while snipping the ripe clusters of the day.

III

Vinification

(This Chapter, as the last, is in part excerpted from THE WINE LOVER'S BIBLE, the first in this series. If the reader has not exposed himself/herself to the first book, this chapter is crucial to understanding modern vinification.)

Traditional vinification, the making of wine from grapes, was once explained to me by an Export Manager in Burgundy. Practiced up until even World War II, the French *vigneron* would crush the grapes with his bare feet and then fill old 55 gallon oak barrels (that presumably had been in the family for generations) with the juice (must). Natural yeasts would launch the fermentation which proceeded on a hot and bubbly course for several days. When the grape sugars had been attacked by the yeasts and the CO_2 had escaped into the atmosphere, this traditional winemaker then sealed the young wine in the same barrel with the barrel head. The wine remained in the barrique until the following summer when the barrels were opened, the wine racked off the pomace (skins) and lies (dead yeast cells), and bottled.

Incroyable!

But true. By today's standards this is most primitive and simply not done. Indeed we barely remember that such practices were normal. How far we have come! Too much extraction of color and the wines get inky and hard on the palate. Too much extraction of tannins making the wine so hard as to attack one's gums--but able to live for decades. At the end of the day, this practice left far too much to chance.

In the late 1990s I was lucky enough to taste from magnum the 1938 Château Mouton Rothschild, the *Premier Grand Cru* from the great commune of Pauillac. The wine was pitch black. Opaque. There was absolutely no sign of age. Now a great Bordeaux such as Mouton after fifteen years will develop from a deep garnet color to having clear watery edges and slight changes toward lighter even rusty color. This is expected and all good. This wine, the 1938, had the color of last year's vintage! I guessed, but was not able to confirm, that the Château was using in 1938 the individual barrique method of fermentation sealing the new wine on the grape pomace in the barrel for a year. The wine may also have been fermented in tanks but then kept on the skins for 40 to 100 days. In any event, the Mouton had lived 50 years and may be lying in the chai still living. The wine itself, I must confess, was dumb, comatose and inexpressive. Not really worth the wait.

pH

pH is how chemists measure acidity and sweetness. Every winemaker desiring a dry wine (no residual sugar) aims for balance. Think of this as liveliness. pH is a measurement of the liveliness of the wine. The great accomplishment of wine is when the wine is not acidic or too overblown with fruit but seamlessly balanced. This balance presents itself as a pleasing rush on the palate. A harmony that is neither acidic nor fruity. The wine is balanced, in one glorious hit on the palate, a memorable experience.

A word on sweet versus fruity. Sweet means the taste of sugar. Fruity does not describe or care about sweetness. Fruity is a description of the momentary or profound essence of fruit in the wine, not sweetness. The wine can "speak" grape, pineapple, grapefruit, cherry, raspberry, melon, etc. These fruit descriptions (or 'descriptors') aim at well known tastes that the wine tasting experience resembles in a bone dry wine. This is a real hurdle for many wine beginner tasters—being able to separate sweetness from fruit flavors. Learn to separate the two. Perhaps two thousand people in my presence have tasted bone dry wine and exclaimed: "It's sweet!"

No! It was fruity. After the extraordinary fortune you spent buying this book and my words above *please never confuse sweet with fruity ever again.* This will help me in my life's mission of enabling wine lovers to share the sensory experience of wine.

Wine: How Long a Life Span?

The life of wine has its beginnings as grape juice, is fermented and becomes wine; there follows a slow march to its ultimate death as vinegar (acetic acid). The aging arc therefore is extraordinarily important when one is laying down wines waiting for their peak development. A rule of thumb is to buy a case of Grand Cru Bordeaux, a Bolgheri Cabernet/Syrah blend or Napa Cabernet Sauvignon from a great vintage when the wine is released. Wait three or four years, then drink the first bottle and repeat on the same holiday with the same friends and family year after year. Hardly scientific but much fun over the twelve year life span of that case.

Mise en Bouteille au Château

What does this mean? It means: Bottled at the Château which is a guarantee that the grapes were grown and the wine made from vines at the Château. And that the wine was vinified at the Château and bottled at the Château: 'This is the wine of this Château and we guarantee it!'

This may seem overly obvious but before World War II wines were shipped in bulk by ship to Paris and London for bottling. This opened the gates for the unscrupulous to "water down" the wine with bulk wines of inferior quality—cheap wine from Algeria, Languedoc or Rousillon—or even with water enhancing the bottler's bottom line.

Modern Winemaking

Winemakers like to think of themselves as poets of the grape but they are also microbiologists with much time spent in the lab.

Yeast cultures: how doth one encourage crushed grapes to become wine? One way, the natural way, is to ferment with the wild yeasts present on the harvested grape direct from the vineyard. When there are not sufficient naturally occurring yeasts on the grape cluster, the winemaker is faced with a problem: juice (or must) that has not gone dry. This is known as a "stuck" fermentation. The yeasts have not been sufficient to eliminate all the grape sugars. Then the winemaker must turn to yeasts cultured in the lab. This move to cultured yeasts is a necessity to nudge crushed juice onward to ferment dry. A wine with sugars not fermented leaves the winemaker with carbon dioxide bound in the must, the possibility of a secondary fermentation taking place in the bottle and volatile acidity in the form of bacteria munching on the sugars and causing foul orders and delivering a wine to the public that is somewhat sweet and unbalanced. And poised for terrible off flavors. Mantra: ferment all wines bone dry!

The pH of your palate yearns for perfectly balanced wine. Do not drink a sweet soda just prior to a glass of wine. The wine will taste 'yuk' because of the lingering sugar from the soda pop. Your personal pH, the pH on your palate, will not be conducive to tasting wine.

Review: Vinification simply put is the fermentation of crushed ripe grapes to gain a level of final alcohol content between 9-16% by volume. The process is inaugurated by yeast (wild or cultured). The yeast attacks the grape sugars producing a hot and tumultuous bubbling vat, released CO_2 and a result is a wine with a particular alcohol content delivered by the grapes' sweetness level. What was juice has become wine. The fermentation of a dry wine is complete when the yeasts have attacked virtually all the sugars. The CO_2 dissipates into the atmosphere and the wine temperature drops to the ambient temperature. The dead yeasts (they die when there is no more sugar to attack) settle to the bottom of the tank. Grape juice has become wine.

Some winemakers endeavor to only use wild yeasts. Others will kill off the wild years by dusting the clusters with sulfur at the de-stemmer-crusher and then inoculate the crushed grapes with lab yeasts. Which are best—wild yeasts or cultured yeasts? *Chacon à son gout!*

Some regions (Germany, Austria, Alsace, Switzerland, and Chablis) do not have the heat summation days during the growing season to get their grapes higher than 17 or 18 degrees Brix. These are wines of finesse, not power. They can also be exceedingly simple.

As mentioned earlier, Brix is a measure of sugar solids in a grape. One can halve (without total accuracy) the Brix number to guess at the eventual alcohol by volume after the fermentation has gone dry, i.e. when the yeasts have done their swimming around in search of sugar and, having found none, expire. A Pinot Noir harvested at 23 or 24 Brix may yield a 14% alcohol wine.

In cool growing regions such as Germany, you will find delicate white wines—some a little sweet, some bone dry--rarely surpassing 9-11% alcohol. Because Germany is relatively cool and therefore not enough sugar.

In a wine region where summation of heat days is not a problem, the grapes can ascend to 25 and 27 Brix or higher. And that explains how we get table wines with alcohols higher than 14 per cent alcohol by volume. High levels of sugar through photosynthesis gained in the vineyard produces sweet grapes and—after fermentation--high alcohol but a dry wine.

Chaptalization

A higher final alcohol can be achieved by Chaptalization which is a method of adding beet or cane sugar to the fermentation. American marketers refer to this practice pejoratively as 'sunshine in a bag'. The practice was introduced in the 19th Century to French winemakers by the chemist Jean-Antoine Chaptal. This method does elevate alcohol however subtracts somewhat from fruit character because the wine has been diluted. Stability and travel-ability can be stunted—a phenomenon known as 'bottle shock'. The wine is now composed of fermented grapes plus fermented cane or beet sugar and though these wines can be fine and delicate, they lack power to some degree with ten percent or so of the alcohol having come from the added (flavorless) cane or beet sugar.

In 1990 I witnessed the workers at the great Château Latour in Pauillac dumping sugar bags into the fermenting tanks despite the fact that the earth was cracked and parched because of an unusually hot growing season. Why oh why I asked are you adding sugar? "We always do it" was the straightforward answer I got. The practice, at Château Latour anyways, had become a tenet comparable to a religious ritual

But the result of Chaptalization is excellent for winemakers in microclimates of low heat summation days during the growing season. Germany, Chablis, Alsace, Austria and Switzerland are not warm climates. But they are capable of making wines of real finesse while using Chaptalization.

California does not allow the addition of cane or beet sugar however allows the addition, as the winemaker deems necessary, of concentrated grape juice to increase alcohol in the fermentation process. This is a rare practice in California which has ample sunshine and where significant rainfall between April bud break and a September or October harvest is usually minimal.

Italy, unlike France, does not add sugar to elevate alcohols. It's warm enough in Italy to avoid this intervention.

I do recall a Napa vintner who had a crop of Chardonnay that did not get picked in a timely manner because of a shortage of labor. He was small and got only late attention from the Mexican crews. Because of the delay, his vineyard attained too high a level of sugar and considerable *botrytis cinerea,* the noble rot. He finally got the vineyard picked, added more sugar in the form of grape concentrate, then had to add water (illegally!) and yet won a gold medal in the dessert wine category at the Orange County Fair. Go figure. (I will not tell you his name; don't ask.)

Gravity

To avoid the 'bruising' of crushed juice (must) that pumping can involve while transporting juice through hoses from the crusher to the fermentation tanks to barrels and then on to the bottling line, modern wineries are being designed to permit the juice to travel by gravity from crusher down to a lower level where the fermentation tanks are located and then even lower to the barrel aging room. This is a practice at the high end of wine quality.

Prohibition Era

During Prohibition, American home winemakers could buy grapes and made up to 200 gallons per household each year! This is a good example of how Congress will submit to many amendments in order to satisfy all and eventually to pass a bill. The 'home wine' provision satisfied many immigrants! In a winery, sacramental wine was the only wine that could be made legally during Prohibition. So the California grape shippers were careful to post notices on the grape crates: "Do not crush these grapes and add yeast as this will cause a fermentation with the result being an illegal wine." Clever fellows with a good understanding of Freedom of Speech! So whole boxcars of grapes went east during Prohibition sent by the Mondavis and the Gallo brothers from the Lodi region and elsewhere. For home winemakers.

Not every drop, to be sure, was consumed at the dinner table.

Tannin

In red wine you will find up to 13 tannic compounds that are acids. Tannin can be best be understood, as a feeling evidencing itself on the palate as an astringent or drying character. Because there is no taste to tannin, only feeling. All wine, of course, as discussed earlier has acids from the time the grapes are tiny nuggets after shatter and the formation of clusters. But young red wines can be simply too tannic and cause unpleasant scratchiness on the roof of the mouth and the tongue. This will be caused by picking immature grapes that have not attained a high enough sugar content (remember Brix) to balance the acidity of the wine with fruitiness. And even a well timed picking and crushing may yield a tannic wine if it is not allowed to age a year or three. Aging allows the wine tannins to cling to leaf and branch particles and fall out as sediment. Aeration (exposing the wine to oxygen) of the young wine in the winery also helps reduce tannin. But some wines, like those of Bordeaux in the poor vintage of 1975, will never lose their tannic character. Too much tannic acidity in the bottle? And too little fruit? There's no place to hide. You own that tannic wine forever. Aging a wine can only do so much.

Most wineries hold back release of young reds until the tannins have softened. (Once again: aeration is becoming a common technique to soften wine.) Sediment is largely bits of stems, branches, leaves, skins and other material in a wine that have attached to tannins and fallen out. Sediment is a beneficial and natural occurrence.

Sur lie Aging

Yeasts die during fermentation. When there are no sugars left to attack they expire. What happens then after the yeasts have swum about the fermentation attacking sugar and creating alcohol as a by-product? These dead critters fall to the bottom of the fermentation vessel and the wine is subsequently racked off the dead lies (pronounced lees like many men named Lee). Rather than being racked off and separated from the still wine, the lies in a still white wine can be stirred, mechanically or by hand, with a baton or paddle (the practice is called *batonnage*) to bring the lies into contact with the wine. This is *sur lie* aging and the practice is done throughout the world. White wine makers may as a matter of style and skill stir the dead yeasts in the post-fermentation vessel giving their wines a degree of creaminess. Many winemakers go a step further and collect the silt that is the dead yeasts and sell such in powder form to chefs as that wonderful cooking ingredient cream of tartar. The next time you drink Muscadet *sur lie* from the Loire Valley, think of the dead yeasts--who have given up their brief lives to bring about alcoholic conversion--that are now contributing to the wine's soft creaminess.

Secondary Fermentation

All red wines following or during primary fermentation are inoculated with lactic acid bacteria which convert naturally present malic acid to lactic acid. This step reduces tartness. It has become common for Chardonnay producers to introduce this secondary fermentation to reduce the apple-like tartness of malic acid, reducing total acidity by about half, resulting in lactic acid which contributes a creamy texture and taste. The winemaker may take the step with a small percentage of the vintage or the entire vintage depending on the particular style sought. Ever taste milk or cream in a Chardonnay? This is how it got there.

From Wine to Vinegar

Wine is that wonderful beverage consumed at a level of ripeness between the mature grape just picked and the wine's eventual demise as vinegar. Tired and exhausted, a victim of slow oxidation it has become wine vinegar, that acidic liquid we use in salads to counter and balance the rich fattiness of mayonnaise or the sweetness of fruit. This move to vinegar can be induced by a

Mother of Vinegar—bacteria that attack the wine's alcohol and reduce it to acetic acid. Needless to say, you do not expect the bottle of wine you just bought to have moved to a vinegar state. Rather you purchase delicious, drinkable wine at a time between the ripe, uncrushed grape and vinegar stages.

Sulfur

Why are American wine labels printed with "Contains sulfur"? Simply because the Bureau of Alcohol, Tobacco and Firearms mandates such information. (Or BATF as it is commonly known and now contained within the Department of Homeland Security.) This regulation for labeling came about to inform people who cannot tolerate high sulfurs which can cause all sorts of pulmonary difficulties some even fatal. The highest incidence of sulfur is usually found in dried fruits. The sulfur in dried fruits has been added to retard spoilage. It can be present at a level as high as 400 parts per million.

But in Europe, no such label requirement exists. This has kicked off a bit of a harmless nationalistic pissing match. European wine marketers will challenge California wine representatives with "So why do you put sulfur in your wines?" Implying, of course, that they are holy and above such a practice.

The truth is that no wine is free of some level of sulfur. Sulfur is a byproduct of fermentation. Always. It can also occur from sulfur residue following the rinsing of previously employed barrels. The cleaning with a sulfur solution or sulfur sticks that are lighted in the barrels as they are being recycled for the next vintage is normal and is done in order to assassinate any microbial life in the barrel. Such microbial life that remains may well rocket the wine into the undrinkable category, even to its arrival as early vinegar. This is what is known as Volatile Acidity, i.e. microbial (bacterial) presence in wine that can cause a secondary activity that fouls the wine taste. Ironically VA can also produce some lovely palate notes.

Another source of traces of sulfur is sulfur introduced to harvested grapes to kill off native years (and other critters) at the time of crushing just before the alcoholic fermentation is started with cultured years.

Also, in rainy vintages, the winemakers may have the crews in the field spraying the vines with a sulfur solution to prevent bunch rot. As molds love warm humid weather to grow, this sprayed sulfur retards their spreading. Such spraying of the vines can leave traces of sulfur.

Sulfur traces retard your nose and therefore your palate. Amen. Light a match in the bathroom and you have not destroyed bathroom odor. What you have done is affected your sense of smell so that the noxious odor seems to have disappeared. In truth, a person's sense of smell is temporarily shut down in the presence of sulfur.

Wineries have made great strides in limiting sulfur in wine. As recently as the 70s I encountered up to 50% of French wine and 10-20% of California wines with noticeable sulfur odor upon opening the bottle. Now it's very rare from either country. The consumers screamed and the winemakers listened.

Today it is rare to find a wine with more than one hundred parts per million of sulfur and 50 parts per million is seen as normal. Dried apricots can contain up to 400 parts per million and cause death in some highly susceptible people. But wine is no long seen as any kind of danger from sulfur. This is the Golden Age of Wine. It has *never* been better.

Barrel Aging

Fifty-five gallon French oak barrels are principally made of wood harvested from the Nevers and Allier forests in France. The oak trees are carefully protected by French law and permits to cut are doled out to restrain human greed in the name of future generations. The French furniture makers also lust the oak of these forests. American coopers purchase French oak (in the form of aged staves) directly from France or get native oak from the forests of Missouri and Kentucky. The American oaks are different varieties but quite similar to the French. There are also 2,000 gallon *tonneaux* typically made of chestnut that are utilized to age and therefore soften wine in less expensive wine regions. These are common in Italy. The extracted flavor components in wood, oak especially, can impart warm textures and complementary virtues. There are vanilla characters and burnt charcoal toasty flavors that are charming in new oak but these dissipate after a few years and integrate. Barrel aging offers a time of rest for the wine, a time to leach flavors from the wood, and time to clean itself by letting skin solids settle. After, the wine can be periodically drawn off the barrel leaving the sediment behind. This is called racking.

Barrels breathe. There is perhaps a 5% loss of wine volume as small water and alcohol molecules penetrate the staves over a year's time while the wine rests in barrel. This is called 'the angels share' and the reason why barrel rooms (or *chai*) smell so delicious!

In the case of Chardonnay, what a marriage! Fermentation in oak barrels and aging in oak barrels make

Chardonnay much better. However, many California winemakers in the 1970s followed the Texas maxim "Too much ain't enough" with the oak aging of their Chardonnay and are still trying to live down the over-oaking image that many folks pinned on them. The honey, vanilla and almond characters of new oak can, if the barrels are judiciously used during fermentation and aging, can take Chardonnay to the stars.

You need to know that the great percentage of table wines never are kissed by wood aging vessels rather only see stainless steel fermentation tanks or concrete tanks with polymer linings from the time of crush to the bottle.

New French Oak barrels (2015) are now demanding up to $1,000 per barrel. You, the ultimate consumer, pay this price.

Corked Wines

The awful taste of a corked wine (*bouchonée* to the French) is one of life's gross offenses. Chemists will tell you that the villain is a virus 2,4,6-trichloroanisole (TCA) or 2,4,6-tribromoanisole (TBA) that existed in the bark as a uninvited virus when stripped from the tree. The wine is decidedly non-commercial and you have every right to return the bottle to the retailer or the waiter and ask for another. Or a refund. Screw caps are free of this malady and are rapidly being utilized for more and more table wines.

Will corks be replaced by composite closures or screw caps? It's too early to tell.

Sediment

Sediment occurs naturally. It consists of particles of grape skins and other solids in the wine attaching to acids and falling to the bottom of the bottle naturally softening the wine. For the most part, storing fine wines on their sides with the wine resting against the cork, allows sediment to collect over a period of years on the side of the bottle and decanting will do the rest when you are ready to carefully pour the treasured wine for dinner.

Most commercial wines are heavily filtered, and fined, stripping away skin particles and other odd particles like pieces of branches and leaves. This results in "a thousand points of light" as George H.W. Bush was famously quoted (but not about wine), resulting in a shiny, translucent glass of wine. No sediment will ever visit these wines.

Filtration

Before bottling, both red and white wines for the most part, are filtered. This removes solid particles from branches and skins remaining after fermentation and aging. The most common filtering agent is diatomite, a porous rock with fine particles. This "dust" or diatomaceous earth coats a metal filter and then wine is forced through leaving undesirable solids behind. And voila! A translucent wine.

Fining

Fining is yet another way of "cleaning up" wines to remove odd solids and leave a thoroughly translucent product. Some of the fining agents used by winemakers are Isinglas (for whites) and egg whites (for reds).

Isinglas is a collagen made (you may find this strange) from the bladders of fish; cod is the most common source, sometimes sturgeon.

Another fining method, but only for red wines, is the addition of egg whites which are separated from yolks and then stirred into the wine barrels during aging. The odd undesirable solids adhere to the egg whites and clean up the wine. The egg whites are racked off following their use and do not become in any way part of the wine. Some wineries trade the unused yolks with bakeries in return for bread and cake!

A cloudy, unfiltered and/or unfined wine delivers more flavor. But this very cloudiness is seen as a negative in the marketplace by many consumers except to the initiated. Mr.

Retailer does not like wine returned because the customer—pointing at the cloudiness—insists that the wine has gone 'bad'.

I recommend that you buy such naturally-made free of industrial influence, cloudy wines, whether unfined or unfiltered or both and cellar them and wait until the moment is right to decant the wine and enjoy. Unfiltered and/or unfined wines will throw off more sediment eventually but they will taste richer.

Reverse Osmosis

The longer black grape clusters are left on the vines, the more chance the skins have to add and develop Anthocyanins which are pigments, the color components of grape skins. This is good, right? The more developed the skin color, the richer the wine? Yes. It's true. Unfortunately, more alcohol is produced because of higher Brix reading of 28-29 which will push the wine alcohol over 16.5% and up. This elevation of the alcohol may even yield wine above the legal limits of alcohol mandated for table wines as defined by the national wine authorities. High alcohol wines may also offend the nose making the wine resemble strong spirits; you will not experience a wondrous bouquet but rather the high alcohol content may cause the wine to smell like vodka.

Many wines in the modern era are made in the 14-15.5% alcohol range without smelling like alcohol. This is because the superior fruit of these wines can support high alcohol levels. Without smelling like a distilled brandy, vodka or 80 proof gin.

Patience please. This longish prologue is getting you, my reader, to Reverse Osmosis.

Reverse osmosis is a technique developed by the Australians. Leaving the grapes in the vineyard advances the skin color but also advances the alcohol content by pushing Brix (remember this gauge of sugar solids?) into 26-29 Brix readings. These grapes of intense color need to be altered to be commercial; the wines need a lower alcohol level. To accomplish this, the winemakers force the wine through filters. The filters push through alcohol and water, the smallest molecules in wine.. Skin molecules, tannins and most of the acidity remain behind. They then distill the water and alcohol separating them. Alcohol volatilizes quickly when heated. Then they reintroduce the water to the wine. Not much is lost in terms of volume and your Australian Shiraz from New South Wales (Hunter Valley), Victoria State (Yarra) or South Australia (Coonawarra, Barossa, Clare, McLaren Vale) will display deep color and flavor without the negatives of high alcohol. This is a significant contribution to making wines of intense flavor. This is a commercial process. Not natural. But it works. They have sunshine in Australia. Lots of it. But they are in danger of using up the water supply but that's another story. Reverse osmosis, also used in beer production, is pretty clever. Reverse osmosis is a friend to mass produced wines. And the wines are very reasonably priced.

Acidulation

Acidulation is the exact reverse of Chaptalization. Flabby overblown, too sweet grapes are going to be over the top in terms of fruitiness. The little original nuggets (looking like BBs) were very acidic when the clusters were being formed. But in the vineyard, the heat resulted in so much photosynthesis that the fruit sugars far surpassed the acid. Result: flab! Over the top fruitiness. What to do? Add acid. Usually citric or tartaric acid are chosen when acidulating. The winemaker adds acid and gets the pH back in balance and everything is fine? Maybe. An experienced palate will detect the monkeying around with Mother Nature involved with the practice of acidulation. An experienced wine taster will judge the wine as an indifferent commercial product. Good tasters can recognize quickly which wines have been acidulated. Good experienced tasters can also experience which wines have been Chaptalized. Make this a goal of your wine tasting life---be able to detect acidulation and Chaptalization. It's an advanced level of wine experience but attainable. Specifically, it is the detection of the natural versus the artificial. To do this one must trust the moment. One must remember the natural explosive and exciting rewards on the palate of fine wine and one must remember unnatural elements superimposed atop the natural. Think Splenda versus sugar. Think Coca Cola versus orange juice.

    Practice will get you there.

IV

Tuscany

Let me begin the story of Tuscany with two families, both descended from nobility: Frescobaldi and Antinori. Both are families with huge vineyard holdings, both families are descended from nobility and both have grown their legacies while entering the age of globalism.

Piero Antinori made his family name known throughout the world. He did it with great wines which gave the name the necessary luster to flood supermarkets shelves with table wines.

Antinori's Fattoria Aldobrandesca is located in the southern part of the Tuscan Maremma, or Bolgheri, right in the center of what is called "the Etruscan zone of tufaceous rock". Here are produced some of the greatest Cabernet Sauvignon based wines of the world. The vineyards of the Fattoria Aldobrandesca are situated right on a spur of tufaceous rock, surrounded by a lovely panorama of real archeological interest as well. The estate was purchased by the Antinori family in 1995 and extends for over 193 total hectares (more than 480 acres) on a gently descending plain of volcanic origin. The property is approximately 650 feet above sea level.

In Bolgheri Piero Antinori also owns the Guado al Tasso estate which makes "Super Tuscan" wines.

Ornellaia in Bolgheri was founded by an Antinori cousin in 1981--Lodovico Antinori. In 1999 Robert Mondavi and the Frescobaldi bought the holding as a joint venture. This is 'Super Tuscan' wine of the highest order.

Antinori also owns the Santa Cristina estate near Cortona. The estate was launched in 2006. Another property Badia a Passignano is located in Chianti Classico. A Riserva is made. Badia a Passignano Gran Selection is produced exclusively from a selection, like a Reserve, of the estate of the same name. Santa Cristina The venerable Tuscan city of Cortona occupies the peak of a high hill not far from Siena and Perugia. On one side a spacious plain, on the other the hill and the city itself. This is the view which can be enjoyed from the new Santa

Cristina cellars, constructed in 2006, 60 years after the first production in 1946, to confirm and renew the tradition of the wines of the same name.

In Brunello di Montalcino, Antinori owns Pian delle Vigna where the vineyard slopes reach down to the train station of Montalcino.

Antinori is a 'negociant' too buying grapes and wine in many regions of Italy and commercialized under the Antinori name.

Stag's Leap Wine Cellars in Napa Valley was purchased from Warren Winiarski by Piero Antinori along with Chateau Saint Michelle of Washington state in 2007 for almost $200 million.

The Frescobaldi are a prominent Florentine noble family that have been involved in the political, sociological, and economic history of Tuscany since the Middle Ages. As bankers, the Frescobaldi financed ventures for numerous members of European royal families, notably their financial conquest of England, which Fernand Braudel has signaled as the greatest achievement of the Florentine firms, "not only in holding the purse-strings of the kings of England, but also in controlling sales of English wool which was vital to continental workshops and in particular to the *Arte della Lana* of Florence."

Frescobaldi have the largest vineyard holdings in Tuscany. It is said that the Frescobaldi buy but never sell. Their estates are as follows.

Castelgiocondo is a southwest facing vineyard estate planted in Sangiovese Grosso which is normal in Brunello di Montalcino. They also make a Merlot here called Lamaione.

The Nipozzano estate in Chianti Rufina makes a Chianti Classico Riserva of excellence from estate vines to the east of Florence and at an elevation surpassing 1000 feet.

They own 50% of Ornellaia in Bolgheri along with Robert Mondavi Winery since 1999.

Tenuta Frescobaldi di Castiglioni, a Super Tuscan, is located in Chianti and the blend is 50% Cabernet Sauvignon, 30% Merlot, 10% Cabernet Franc and 10% Sangiovese.

In the tiny Pomino estate Frescobaldi make an excellent Pinot Noir, which is an exception in itself in Italy, labeled Pomino Rosso blended with small amounts of Sangiovese and Merlot.

Tuscany has 157,000 acres planted to grapes; 70% is planted in red varietals and the greater part of this is Sangiovese varietal, a clone or early ancestor of Cabernet Sauvignon. Sixty percent of each vintage is exported. There is a rumor that wine preceded man in Tuscany. Children bypass beer in favor of wine. Smart children.

Firm rule number 1 in Tuscany: Tuscany is for red wine. The white grapes Trebbiano and Pinot Grigio do not occupy a warm place in my heart. But these two white wines are inexpensive and ubiquitous. Once upon a time it was common to hear: 'Give me a glass of Chablis.' That morphed to: 'Give me a glass of Chardonnay.' Now it's 'Give me a glass of Pinot Grigio.' Perhaps next will be: 'Give me a glass of Trebbiano.'

Sangiovese is a relative of Cabernet Sauvignon. We can safely say that Cabernet is the clone having morphed over the centuries to the form dominating Bordeaux and now loved throughout the world. Sangiovese has a different profile. Cabernet Sauvignon on the palate is prepossessing: like walking into an immense mansion if you are drinking a great one, with many rooms large and small, hallways and openings like windows to a world of pleasure. Sangiovese, the Tuscan cousin, is more of a glass smooth river with ripples not waves. This river runs deep, a friendly river giving the taster a sense of a wide pleasant world.

This is the grape that dominates the vineyards of Chianti which extend from mountainous Rufina on the east, south past Siena to the very borders of the mountain town Montalcino. On the north, Chianti ends just past Florence; on the west portions extend to Bolgheri and the Tyrrhenian Sea.

One absolutely must have their arms around the regions of Tuscany both to be able to buy with intelligence and also with respect to learning the 'typicity' of each region of Tuscany. The following regions are described both in terms of typicity and the wine laws of Italy which maintain geographical integrity for the sourcing of wines.

Chianti is the largest region within Tuscany. Historically the area made red wines of 70% Sangiovese that included 15% Trebbiano (a white) and 15% Canaiolo and/or Malvasia (reds). This blending was sacrosanct from the middle of the 19th century until traditions started to tumble in the late 1970s. Since 1996 the blend for Chianti and Chianti Classico has been 75–100% Sangiovese, up to 10% Canaiolo and up to 20% of any other approved red grape variety such as Cabernet Sauvignon, Merlot or Syrah.

This represents a huge departure from traditional blending which kept Chianti from making the quality that the area was capable of. Since 2006, the use of white grape varietals such as

Malvasia and Trebbiano have been prohibited in Chianti Classico. Few producers still package their wines wrapped in straw *(fiaschi)* that forever provided candle holders for college dormitories throughout the western world.

I asked a famous Chianti Classico Riserva winemaker why Chianti had for so long diluted their red wine with simple Trebbiano. His frank reply: "It was the only way we could get rid of it."

But first a little defining of the appellation information found on Tuscan labels. Stay with me. It's an alphabet soup but necessary to know.

Chianti DOC *Denominazione di origine controllata.* Controlled designation of Origin. Meaning that the grapes in this wine come from the area—in this case Chianti.

DOCG *Denominazione di Origine Controllata e Garantita.* This is a slightly higher promise of provenance--Controlled Destination is Guaranteed. Why a promise upon a promise? Why did controlled morph to Guaranteed Controlled? The truth is the

Italians are fighting a legacy of cheating. In France vintners will say: 'We have a few cheats here and there but in Italy: "*Mon dieu, how they cheat!*"

IGT *Indicazione Geografica Tipica.* IGT on the label references the source of the grapes but not the more restrictive DOC and DOCG rules as to vines within a prescribed land mass. This classification was introduced in the early 1990s. Antinori broke the rules (thank you Marchese!) when he deviated from the historical Chianti restrictions. He labels his excellent and high priced Tignanello and Solaia: Toscana IGT. Which guarantees that the wine is Tuscan in origin and bears a typicity that is Tuscan. But with non-native Cabernet Sauvignon in the blend. This caused a rift in sleepy Italy. The wine was great. The fame would rub off on all producers. They simply had to come up with a face-saving category. IGT is that category.

Producers throughout Chianti since the 1980s have adopted modern practices. In the vineyards they pick later in the season hoping to have the 'fruit forward' character best exemplified in the

New World wines and popular with the wine public. Leanness and crisp acidity are out of favor. The Tuscan have invested in trellising to give the clusters equal access to the sun. Many have adopted mechanical harvesting. And they have--importantly-- invested in small barrique, for the most part French in provenance that have elevated the wines from simple to world class.

Chianti DOC is the base level of Chianti quality. Good. Cheap. Ubiquitous. Such wines can include some grapes from the Chianti Classico region but the labeling cannot reveal this.

Chianti Superiore DOC is produced around the Tuscan cities and villages of Arezzo, Florence, Pisa, Pistoia, Prato and Siena. This is inexpensive wine that can be sold after only one year with three months of that (counted from January 1) year guaranteed to have been in bottle. The wine may contain some grapes from the Chianti Classico Region—but this cannot be mentioned on the label. Time in oak? Anyone's guess.

Chianti Riserva DOC spends two years in oak and minimum of three months in the bottle. Minimum of 75% Sangiovese. The 'step down' in price here is that the grapes are not from the Classico zone. Less expensive but in many cases the aging is significant on the palate.

Chianti Classico DOCG These wines can be released after two years. They probably have seen time in large chestnut tonneau but 55 gallon French oak barrique? Probably not.

The Chianti Classico zone takes up about 25% of the Chianti region and stretches roughly from Florence in the north to Siena in the south. These wines may be quite a quality step up from simple Chianti. Along with a minimum of 80% Sangiovese, other red grapes of the area can be blended in. These grapes include natives like Canaiolo and Colorino as well as Cabernet Sauvignon, Merlot and Syrah. The wines from a great vintage can be very good. From a so-so vintage they are just okay. These wines are released relatively young, at age two, and young wines can have a bite. They have not had the chance to soften. But they are less expensive.

Chianti Classico Riserva represents about 20% of the production of the Chianti Classico zone each vintage year. Historically there was no guarantee of time in oak barrels, time in the bottle or any other special quality. Additionally the wines were not permitted to be released for sale for three years. However now you can bank on a Riserva being a minimum of 80% Sangiovese from the Chianti Classico region and the wine has aged for a minimum of two years before release for sale. The consumer needs to find a Brand that consistently delivers excellence. Five to seven years after an excellent vintage year, these wines can be extraordinary. Some will live 20 years and develop more and more complexity during two decades. The softness achieved with extended aging is remarkable in Riservas. The nose is particular to Tuscany and a great pleasure on the palate.

Noted producers: Badia a Coltibuono; Monsanto; Ruffino; Castellare; Castello dei Rampolla; Isole e Olena; Melini; Banfi; Badia a Passignano (Antinori); Villa Antinori.

Chianti Rufina DOCG is a small mountainous region to the east of Florence at 1000' elevation (more or less due to the mountainous character) and is situated above the hilly valley floor of Chianti Classico. Nights are cooler and the growing season is longer producing deeper skin color due to longer time on the vine. Frescobaldi produces a Chianti Classico Rufina Riserva from its Castello di Nipozzano estate that is superior to many wines on the valley floor below. With 500 acres planted, the wine shows a refined richness due to the coolness of the higher elevation.

Taste Chianti Classico Rufina along with Chianti Classico from the lower hills and you may well choose the Rufina wine. But it is a small area and Rufina (not to be confused with the Ruffino family winery) wines are not ubiquitous.

Noted Producers: Fattoria Selvapiana; Castello di Nipozzano (Frescobaldi).

Vernaccia di San Gimignano DOC In the northwest of Tuscan lays this white wine region. The Vernaccia grapes produce a delightfully fruity wine and the winemakers leave a touch of carbonation in the wine resulting in a slight spritzy (or *frizzante*) character. An unusual wine you will find delightful.

Brunello di Montalcino DOCG This region surrounds the fortified mountain town of Montalcino. The grapes are 100% a clone of Sangiovese: Sangiovese Grosso--large black skinned grapes (locally called Prugnolo) that in a hot non-rainy vintage are not picked until October. The grape skins provide extraordinary coloring guaranteeing long life. The vineyards for the most part look to the southwest to gain the benefit of the late afternoon sun. The wines are among the best in the world but are expensive. Prices start at about $50 and many exceed $100.

Luce delle Vita is a joint venture by Robert Mondavi and the Marchesi di Frescobaldi. (Generally the first born male is called Marchese; the Frescobaldi name all the sons Marchesi to perhaps extend the nobility as they market the Brand name throughout the world. Wine lovers in general adore nobility!)The first wines were released from the 1993 and 1994 vintages which were mediocre. But the 1995-1997 vintages were spectacular. The Sangiovese grapes in this wine hail from (potentially from other vineyards also) the Frescobaldi Castelgiocondo estate and sometimes are blended with Merlot.

Noted Producers of Brunello di Montalcino: Altesino; Banfi; Barbi; Biondi Santi Jacopo-Tenuta Greppo (requires a minimum of 15 years aging); Casanova di Neri; Castelgiocondo (Frescobaldi); Caparzo; La Gerla; Mocali; Pian delle Vigna (Antinori); Poggio Antico; Tenute Silvio Nardi; and Uccelliera.

Rosso di Montalcino DOC wines are grown in Brunello di Montalcino vineyards. Why? There are several potential and/or actual reasons. The Rosso requires only one year of aging before release. While Brunello is a five year affair before release. Also the decision to release their wine as Rosso di Montalcino can be a result of cash flow needs or simply that the vintage is not up to expectation and the winery is protecting its name from a portion of the vintage not up to 'snuff'. There are also worldwide slowdowns in sales as happened following the economic collapse of 2008. Marking a wine down from $100 to $30 can be a most wise and necessary decision. Good for the buyer!

Vino Nobile di Montepulciano DOCG is a blended red wine produced in the vineyards surrounding the town of Montepulciano in the southeast region of Tuscany The wine is made primarily from the Sangiovese grape varietal (known locally as Prugnolo gentile) minimum 70%, blended with Canaiolo Nero (10%–20%) and small amounts of other local varieties such as Mammolo. The wine is aged in oak barrels for 2 years; three years if it is a Riserva. A common mistake: The wine is not Montepulciano d'Abruzzo, a red wine made from the Montepulciano grape (not Sangiovese) in the Abruzzo region of east-central Italy.)

Young, these wines can have a certain lively brightness that differs from Chianti though the blending is similar. Aging reduces the youthful brightness but there is a payoff in added complexity at 5-8 years past the vintage date.

Recommended Producer: Avignonesi.

Bolgheri

For the wine lover, Bolgheri is magical. There are vineyards all over Tuscany, often in close proximity to each other, but there certainly are other crops. But in the tiny region of Bolgheri there seems to be virtually nothing else. In Bolgheri, rather like the Côte d'Or in Burgundy, it is wine first and everything else a very poor second.

What is all the fuss about? First, we need to remember that the reputation of Italian wines in the 1960s was, to put it politely, cheap and cheerful. At that time, quality wine was seen as coming from France, cheap plonk came from the Italy. Fine wine in Tuscany came from the inland hills--Chianti and Montalcino—

while the flat land was good for breeding horses. Up to this point only Rosé had been made here commercially by Antinori, on land which had been marshes in living memory. However, back at the end of the second world war, a Tuscan aristocrat, Marquis Mario Incisa della Rocchetta, who bred racing horses and had estates on the Tuscan coast, decided that he would plant Bordeaux varieties on his family estate. The Marquis had a taste for the wines of the Medoc and he noticed some similarity of maritime climate and soil between the gravel of the Medoc and the coastal plain in Tuscany. The name 'Sassicaia' means 'stony ground'. The first vineyards were planted in 1944 and the Marquis matured his wines in small barrels (barriques) on the French model, to the amazement of his workers. Surely wine was made to be drunk before the next harvest came in?

The most common image of the Maremma (or Bolgheri) is that of a maritime zone, one of plains and pine groves, horses and cowboys. The Maremma that we are dealing with here, instead, is the inland part, one which has the indisputable charm of tuff (volcanic rock), the bluffs on which sat, in ancient times, a number of outright fortresses.

Much in the wine world is static. Waiting to taste the next vintage of Corton-Charlemagne from Burgundy only means: 'How will the present differ from the past in quality?' Or. 'How does the new Bordeaux vintage stack up against history?'

But the appearance of Bolgheri in the far west of Tuscany bordering the Mediterranean and the Tyrrhenian Sea has been like discovering a new planet. Even a new constellation. The wine world seemed fixed. But then Bolgheri was born. Not to take the metaphor too far it's almost like a new love. You look into her (or his) eyes and plumb the depths of her (or his) soul trying to divine this amazing creature you have been introduced to.

Prior to the 1980s Bolgheri was largely cattle land. No more. The current set of DOC regulations for Bolgheri red wines became approved in 1994. Before the creation of this DOC, wines from the area were typically sold under the simpler designations *Vino da Tavola* or IGT Toscana.

Along with Tignanello and Solaia (see Antinori above), Bolgheri established the concept of the 'Super Tuscan', a wine that smashes the traditional rules of Tuscany by using non-native varietals. Bolgheri became an internationally known region following an event in 1974 arranged by the UK wine magazine Decanter where a 6-year-old Sassicaia won over an assortment of Bordeaux wines. Prior to this, Bolgheri had been relatively anonymous producers of ordinary white wines and rosés.

Due to the particular characteristics of the soil and micro climate sunny, dry and moderately windy, the grape varieties of Bordeaux origin tend to thrive, such as Cabernet Sauvignon, Merlot, Cabernet Franc and Petit Verdot.

The famous wines: Sassicaia produced by Tenuta San Guido; Tenuta Dell'Ornellaia the producer of Ornellaia, Ca'Marcanda of Angelo Gaja and Guado al Tasso of Antinori. Among many, many small producers with limited availabilities. The appellation rules determine that in Bolgheri Rosso and Bolgheri Rosé, Sangiovese may be utilized only to a degree of

70%, and in excess of this a wine must be classified IGT. Cabernet Sauvignon from 10 to 80%, Merlot up to 80% and other local red varieties, up to 30%. Rosso must be aged for 24 months.

For Bolgheri Bianco, Tuscan Trebbiano from 10 to 70%, Vermentino from 10 to 70%, Sauvignon blanc from 10 to 70% and other local white varieties, up to 30%. The volume of white wine over the past decades has plummeted. Finding a white from Bolgheri resembles looking for a Republican in San Francisco.

Noted Producers: Michele Satta; Le Macchiole (unbelievable quality in Cabernet Franc and Merlot); **Ca' Marcanda** (Angelo Gaja's presence in Bolgheri); Campo alla Sughera; Poggio al Tesoro; **Batzella**; Castello di Bolgheri; Giovanni Chiappini; Ornellaia; and Sassicaia (where the quality revolution started).

V

Piedmont

In the late 1970s Robert Mondavi of the Napa Valley visited the Piedmont's emerging star Angelo Gaja. Gaja took Bob Mondavi from neighbor to neighbor talking vineyards and tasting wine. After a couple of hours Mondavi asked: "Can you hear the snoring?" Gaja, whose English at the time was not *molto bene*, didn't answer.

Later Mondavi asked the same question. "Angelo, can you hear the snoring?" That's when Gaja got it. Gaja's neighbors, the famous producers of Barbaresco and Barolo, were all asleep--and snoring.

Neither Gaja nor Bob Mondavi have ever been accused of snoring by anyone. Gaja's hero in the wine world became Bob Mondavi.

The Gaja winery was founded in 1859 by Giovanni Gaja, the Gaja family having arrived from Spain during the 17th century.

The family Gaja opened a tavern in Barbaresco, serving its wines with the food. At the end of the 19th century, Gaja wines were bottled and supplied to the Italian army in Abyssinia (modern Ethiopia).

In 1937, Giovanni Gaja first put the name Gaja in big red letters on his bottles' labels. The firm progressed following World War II as Giovanni Gaja made a significant series of vineyard purchases in terms of scale and vineyard quality. Also cited as an important influence to the firm's early success is the mother of Giovanni Gaja, Clotilda Rey, Angelo Gaja's grandmother, who instilled the principles of working to achieve high quality to attract the desired clientele, and set high prices to manifest the prestige of the wines.

Angelo Gaja, born in 1940, great-grandson of Giovanni Gaja, began his career with the company in 1961 at the age of 21, having studied wine making at the Enological Institute in Alba and at the University of Montpellier in France, and held a degree in economics from the University of Turin. At the time there were only about 100 wineries producing Barbaresco and Barolo, and Gaja was already the major vineyard owner of Barbaresco.

Following several trips to France and disputes with his father, Angelo Gaja introduced several practices to the region over the following years, revolutionary to the vinification of Nebbiolo. From 1961 began the first experiments with green harvest or *diradamento*, and single vineyard production was started with Sorí San Lorenzo in 1967, Sorí Tildin in 1970 and Costa Russi in 1978. Since 1970 Gaja has employed the eminent oenologist Guido Rivella. Gaja is also credited with introducing to Piedmont malolactic fermentation, from the 1975–1976 vintage implementing French *barriques* ten years after initial experiments, bringing in thermo-controllable fermentation equipment and French grape varieties, and eventually *grand cru* prices. Giovanni Gaja opposed his son's use of new *barriques* and the decision to plant French grape varieties. In 1978 the Darmagi vineyard in Barbaresco, a prime Nebbiolo site, was planted with Cabernet Sauvignon. When Gaja's father learned that Angelo had planted the vineyard in Cabernet Sauvignon he said: "Darmagi!" (Translation: Isn't it a pity!") Today Darmagi sells for $150 per bottle.

Gaja said he planted Darmagi in Cabernet not because of his love for Cabernet Sauvignon but from the belief that only by making a great Cabernet, aged in *barriques*, could he persuade the world that Italy was capable of greatness. And only by succeeding on terms accepted by the rest of the world could he draw attention to the great wines made from Italy's indigenous Nebbiolo.

At the time Pinot Noir from Burgundy and Cabernet Sauvignon from Bordeaux were consider non plus ultra—nothing better—in the world. Today it is pretty much acknowledged that over the top quality wine can be made from Nebbiolo, Sangiovese, Merlot, Syrah, Grenache and a few more.

In 1979 the Gaia & Rey (named after Angelo's son and daughter) vineyard in Treiso was planted with Chardonnay. This is now hands down the finest Chardonnay made in Italy. Later in

1983, Sauvignon Blanc was planted in the Alteni di Brassica vineyard in Barbaresco.

Considered a modernist in a traditional region, Gaja was criticized for his approach in the early years, but unlike many other modernists, Gaja is restricted in the use of new oak. Gaja ferments and leaves his wines on the skins for up to 30 days, the old-fashioned way instead of the modernist 18-20 day time on the skins (maceration) and although he employs *barriques* (⅓ new oak) for the first year of aging, the process is finished in big *botti*-- traditional 10-100+hL casks of Slavonian oak or chestnut some of which are 80–120 years old. Piedmont producers who became inspired by Gaja's methods include Renato Ratti and Aldo Conterno, while Bruno Giacosa is considered by many to be Gaja's "polar opposite".

The reputation of Gaja evolved over the years as his uncompromising policy became established. He refused to sell 12,000 cases of 1984 Barbaresco under the Gaja label, opting instead to sell it off in bulk. And the same was repeated after the distrous vintages of 1992 and 1994. His stature was also strengthened by commendations such as the *Wine Spectator* proclamation that the 1985 Gaja Barbarescos were "the finest wines ever made in Italy", the selection for the 1997 *Wine Spectator* Distinguished Service Award, and for "1998 *Decanter* Man of the Year".

In 1988 Gaja returned to Barolo with the acquisition of 70 acres of property, having previously rented vineyards there and then discontinued the activity when the strategy called for focus on self-owned single vineyards. The Barolo Sperss was first released in 1992. Further acquisitions saw Gaja own property in Montalcino with the Pieve Santa Restituta estate in 1994, Gromis property in La Morra for the production of Barolo Conteisa Cerequio in 1995 and the Ca'Marcanda property in Bolgheri in 1996.

Angelo Gaja has declared he will not expand the firm's holding outside Italy's borders, although in 1989 he came close to a joint venture with the Napa Valley giant Robert Mondavi. He eventually declined, reflecting that it would be "like a mosquito having sex with an elephant: very dangerous and not much pleasure".

Piedmont is surrounded on three sides by the Alps, including Monviso, where the Po rises, and Monte Rosa. It borders with France, Switzerland and the Italian regions of Lombardy, Liguria, Aosta Valley and for a very small fragment with Emilia Romagna. The geography of Piedmont is 43.3% mountainous, along with extensive areas of hills (30.3%) and plains (26.4%).

The best-known fine wines from the region include Barolo and Barbaresco. They are made 100% from the Nebbiolo grape. These wines are ideal for storage and a well-aged Barolo for instance may leave a feeling of drinking velvet because the tannins are polished and integrated more and more into the wine. As the wine matures the color becomes more brownish and rust-red.

Barbaresco is produced in the Piedmont region in an area of the Langhe immediately to the east of Alba. It was granted DOC status in 1966 and *DOCG* status in 1980.

Barolo is a red DOCG also produced in the northern Italian region of Piedmont. It is made from the Nebbiolo grape and is often described as one of Italy's greatest wines. Only vineyards planted in primarily calcareous-clay soils in the hills with suitable slopes and orientations are considered suitable for Barolo production. Barolo is often described as having the aromas of tar and roses, and the wines are noted for their ability to age and usually take on a rust red tinge as they mature. When subjected to aging of at least five years before release, the wine can be labeled a *Riserva*.

In the past, Barolo wines tended to be rich in tannin. It could take more than 10 years for the wine to soften and become ready for drinking. Fermenting wine sat on the grape skins for at least three weeks extracting huge amounts of tannins and was then aged in large, wooden casks for years. In order to appeal to more modern international tastes, those that prefer fruitier, more forward and earlier drinking wine styles, several producers began to cut maceration (time after alcoholic fermentation the new wine is left on the skins) to a maximum of ten days and age the wine in new French oak *barriques*. "Traditionalists" have argued that the wines produced in this way are not recognizable as Barolo and taste more of new oak than of wine. Which is somewhat true. However the vanilla characters of new oak disappear after five to seven years.

The Langhe is a hilly area to the south and east of the river Tanaro in the province of Cuneo in Piedmont. The Nebbiolo grown in Langhe, although outside Barbaresco and Barolo, can be- -in a fantastic vintage--the equal of the two more famous regions. The wise shopper will search out the Langhe wines as they will cost about $20 not $100 or more.

Incidentally this area around Alba is famous for white truffles, a subterranean fungus (a mushroom that grows underground), that lends to pasta with cream sauces a particular and peculiar taste that should be in everyone's bucket list.

Other popular grapes used for red wine production in Piedmont are Barbera and Dolcetto. Wines made on the Barbera grape are often fruity and delicate with less tannin than wine made from the Nebbiolo grape. Barbera, when aged in *barrique,* can improve for 15 years or more. But this is rare.

Dolcetto on the other hand is not as the name indicates sweet. Dolcetto means bright expressive fruit—not sugar. The grape gives fresh and dry red wines with some tannin. The wines made with the Dolcetto grape should be consumed young like Beaujolais—they do not age well. You may also find Bonarda here and there—but not much. Chile and Argentina supply some Bonarda to the US market. Good but rare.

The sparkling wine Asti Spumante (see Chapter XIX: Bubblies and Dessert Wines) is made in the Piedmont region from the Moscato grape. The Brachetto is another variety and is used for making sweet and sparkling red wines.

There's a most interesting white wine made in the Piedmont--Arneis. The wine has bracing acidity--good to pair with rich food--and a flavor profile distinct from any other white wine in Italy. It can be found in the States at specialty retailers at $20 or so.

Piedmont is broadly coincident with the upper part of the drainage basin of the river Po, which rises from the slopes of Monviso in the west of the region and is Italy's largest river

Dolcetto is harvested first, then the Barbera and lastly the Nebbiolo. The countryside is very diversified: from the rugged peaks of the massifs of Monte Rosa and of Gran Paradiso, to the damp rice paddies of Vercelli and Novara, from the gentle hillsides of the Langhe and of Montferrat to the plains.

Although production has grown over the past several decades, Barolo and Barbaresco production remains limited. In 1990 production was perhaps 100,000 cases of 12 bottles. Grand Cru production in Bordeaux that year was ten times higher. Much of the great Piedmontese wine is bought directly by Germans at the various wineries as they drive back home from their summer holiday.

Which is better: Barbaresco or Barolo? This is the kind of somewhat petty argument I prefer to leave to the wine geeks. Rather I prefer simply to say that from a great vintage and aged 10-15 years, both are among the greatest of the world's wines.

Noted Barolo Producers: Elio Altare; Giacomo Fenocchio; Burlotto; Barale Fratelli; Brovia; Roagna, Luigi Einaudi; A.&G. Fantino; Vietti; Ceretto; and Renato Ratti.

Noted Barbaresco Producers: Gaja (pronounced: guy-ah); Produttori Del Barbaresco, a cooperative; Marchesi di Gresy; Ca' del Baio (small); Cantina del Pino (really small); Scarpa; Bruno Giacosa; de Forville; and Falletto.

VI

Veneto

Of all the world's great wines that are generally available to the American and British consumer, I rank the red wines of the

Veneto as the most unknown, most unloved and that great wine which is not regularly considered to compete side by side with the acknowledged greatest wines. This is a pity. The red wines of the Veneto are stellar and may be, dollar for dollar, the best values in the wine world.

However this is changing! The world is getting on to the Veneto. Exports have doubled since 2008. You can fool a lot of individuals but the export markets are stocked with geniuses when it comes to identifying underappreciated wines. Globalism with all its difficulties is working to the benefit of consumers. Trade barriers have been lowered. Delivery systems have benefitted from the Internet. And pressure is put on every region in the world to compete with quality. Certainly Pinot Grigio is responsible for much of the growth in exports but Valpolicella and Valpolicella Ripasso also figure in the growth.

The Veneto is located in north-eastern Italy, one of a group of three highly productive Italian regions known collectively as the *Venezie* (after the ancient Venetian Republic) and is the biggest

DOC producer of the three. Although the Venezie collectively produce more red wine than white, the Veneto region produces more whites under DOC and is home to the famous Soave wines.

The region is protected from the harsh northern European climate by the Alps, the foothills of which form the Veneto's northern extremes. These cooler climes are well-suited to white varieties like Garganega (the main grape for Soave wines) while the warmer Adriatic coastal plains, river valleys, and Garda Lake zone are where the renowned Valpolicella, Amarone and Bardolino DOC reds are produced. In Veneto, two different wine areas are clearly distinguishable: an Eastern part, close to the Venice Lagoon between the hills of Treviso, the plain of Piave river and Adriatic coast, where it is typical to produce the famous Prosecco sparkling wine (the glera grape), and other varieties like Merlot, and Carmenere (which taste very similar and are hard to detect). The traditional trellising system of the eastern part is Sylvoz, is today replaced by the *guyot* (wire trellis) system, while in the western part is more traditionally the Pergola system. The

Pergola system of vine training is common and promotes high yields while sacrificing some quality. However Veneto's growers are among the most modernized in Italy. High demand for Veneto wines in the European and US markets has galvanized the region's producers into experimentation with Cabernets, Chardonnay and Pinot Noir varieties, among others. One of Italy's leading wine schools, Conegliano, is based here and the nation's most important wine fair, Vinitaly, takes place each spring in Verona.

Veneto is the 8th largest region of Italy in land mass, and a population of 4,371,000 ranks it 6th in that regard. It has over 220,000 acres of vineyards, of which 90,000 acres are acclaimed DOC. The Veneto is Italy's largest producer of DOC wine. White wine, and in particular Pinot Grigio, accounts for 55% of the DOC production in Veneto.

You probably have heard nothing of the Corvino grape varietal which is a pity. But it is the base (70-80%) red grape varietal of Valpolicella. Valpolicella Ripasso is a step up: fermented and aged not only with the skins of the grapes just crushed but also the skins of prior fermentations. The added skins, called pomace, produce allow more color and flavor to be extracted. The wines are inky and concentrated. They age very well. This is an extraordinary wine at $20 or more.

Lastly, the greatest wine of the Veneto is Amarone Della Valpolicella DOCG. Also Corvino based but from exceptional vineyards, this wine has depth and aging potential that can taste on the same table with the greatest wines of the world. Amarone tends to be both short in supply but also, somewhat surprisingly, of lesser cost than Grand Cru Burgundy or the classified Growths of Bordeaux in an excellent vintage. But you are still looking in the neighborhood of $60 and as high as $100. As with Barolo and Barbaresco, Amarone is in short supply driving the price up. Amarone is a wine known very well by wine collectors. They know the payoff on the palate when laid down for ten or twenty years.

Any beginner oenophiliac experiencing Amarone for the first time will be, I think, stunned to be suddenly in the presence of greatness.

Noted Valpolicella and Valpolicella Ripasso Producers: Allegrini; Zenato; Bolla; Guerrieri Rizzardi; Corte Majoli; and Antiche Terre.

Noted Amarone Producers: Tenuta Sant'Antonio; Musella; Tommasi; Nicolis; Zenato (produced only in great vintages); and Masi.

VII

Campania

Campania is south of Rome with the largest city being Naples. The land of Mount Vesuvius is latterly getting known as a mountainous area where world class reds are being grown. The two principal growing areas are lofty in altitude: Taurasi and Basilicata. The soils are volcanic and the best slopes face the southwest.

The principal grape is Aglianico. Except for the Taurasi wines of Mastroberardino the region was a black hole of no significance even as late as the 1990s.

There is a brother conflict here perhaps similar to the Mondavi brothers in Napa Valley. The quarrel within the Mastroberardino family resulted in the vineyards staying with one brother and the other creating the Terredora Di Paolo brand. Under the truce agreement the Brand name could no longer be Mastroberardino.

The struggles of family are often linked to the production of fine wine—to the extent that the wines themselves become part of folklore. Great things can come of conflict.

Although in 1992 only the Mastroberardino wines were being exported, everything turned around as that family's fame grew. Although the wines were somewhat rustic, a little coarse and suffering from a lack of modern viticulture and vinification, many of the Mastroberardino wines promised greatness on the global stage.

By 2005 the neighbors had joined into the game: 293 producers were exporting from Taurasi. Why? Because of Campania's Aglianico grape varietal indigenous to the region. By DOC regulation the wine must be 85% Aglianico. What is the future of the Aglianico grape? From this vantage point things look good. With the producers moving from rustic to modern methods and exporting aggressively, competition should reveal whether we will be able to add Aglianico to the pantheon of great varietals. Vineyards must be identified and cultivated to their maximum. The use of oak barrels needs to be understood. And then there comes aging over a long period. There's definitely a chance for Aglianico.

. The region at the end of 2014 had a population of almost six million people, making it the third-most-populous region of

Italy; its total area of 5,247 square miles makes it the most densely populated region in the country.

In the Taurasi zone, the Aglianico grape thrives in vineyards at altitudes of 1,000 to 1,500 feet above sea level. According to DOCG regulations, Taurasi wines must be aged a minimum of 3 years prior to release with at least 1 of those years being in wood. For wines labeled *Riserva*, the wines must be aged for at least 4 years. The wine can be 100% Aglianico, but up to 15% of Piedirosso and Sangiovese may be blended in.

Taurasi and Taurasi Riserva were awarded DOC status in 1970 and DOCG status in 1993. Produced less than 40 miles (64 km) from the other Aglianico stronghold of Aglianico del Vulture in Basilicata, the volcanic soils of the Taurasi region demonstrate the potential the Aglianico grape has to make wines on par with the Nebbiolo grape of Piedmont, the Corvino grape of the Veneto and the Sangiovese grape of Tuscany.

Greco di Tufo is an Italian wine grape that may be of Greek origin. (No surprise as the Romans brought Greek cuttings to the boot.) The name relates to both white (Greco Bianco) and black (Greco Nero) wine grape varieties. While there is more land area dedicated to Greco Nero, the Greco Bianco is the white wine grape most commonly referred to by the shorthand "Greco". In the Campania region it is used to produce the DOCG wine Greco di Tufo. In Calabria, it is used to make DOC wine Greco di Bianco. (Calabria, located just across the water from Sicily, as a separate growing region is not taken up in this book; the region did not fully recover from the phylloxera plague of the late 19th Century.)

As grape vines have been propagated throughout Italy, the name "Greco" has been ascribed to several varieties that may have historically been linked to Greece. Ampelographers disagree about whether Greco is a single variety with several clones or an agglomeration of several varieties under the umbrella name of "Greco". There is also disagreement about whether any of the Italian so-called "Greek vines" are currently being cultivated in Greece.

Noted Producers of the mountainous Taurasi province with volcanic soils: Gioviano; Musto Carmelitano; Salvatore Molettieri; Terredora Di Paolo (formerly Mastroberardino); and Antonio Caggiano.

VIII

Trentino/Alto Adige

The Alto Adige is a vast valley between two mountain ranges: the Alps and the Dolomites. Bozen (Balzano) and Trentino (Trento) are the principal cities. The vineyards lie for the most part on the valley floor and are graced with pergola-trained vines. Much quantity is produced.

Pinot Grigio remains both prolific and simple. An exception to the volume-driven viticulture is the wine of Alois Legeder whose vineyards are wire-trained and small barrique are utilized which adds softness and richness.

Pinot Noir is plentiful too and tends to be thin, light in color and a poor cousin to Burgundy reds. Up against the bold fruit of New World Pinot Noir there is no contest. But the Pinot Noir of the South Tyrol is inexpensive.

Lagrein is a red wine grape variety native to the valleys of South Tyrol and may be a descendant of Teroldego, another South

Tyrol red, and related to Syrah and Pinot Noir. The Lagrein wine tends to be tannic but modern techniques such as the use of oak barrels is adding softness. The price of vineyard land as a repository of wealth is extraordinary. Buying vineyard there is both rare and extremely expensive.

The region was part of Austria-Hungary and its predecessors, the Austrian Empire and the Holy Roman Empire from the 8th century until its annexation by Italy in 1919. Both Italian and German are commonly spoken by the natives. With a past of poverty, the region is today among the wealthiest and most developed in both Italy and the whole European Union.

IX

Sicily

So most of us cannot drink--unless we are billionaires—Barolo, Super Tuscan and Amarone wines every day. Sicily comes to the rescue with an intense and black inky beauty by the name of Nero d'Avola. Under $10 and generally available, this wine give off much satisfaction with little dent on the wallet. This is a red wine with of little complexity but great intensity on the palate.

Sicily is the third largest volume wine producer in Italy after the Veneto and Emilia Romagna. The region is known mainly for fortified Marsala wines more employed in the kitchen for cooking than at the dinner table. The high alcohol in this cooking wine is not a problem. For when exposed to heat, the alcohol volatilizes into the atmosphere.

However in recent decades the wine industry has improved, new winemakers are experimenting with less-known native varietals and Sicilian wines have become better known. Nero d'Avola, named for a small town not far from Syracuse, is the best known. The best wines made with these grapes come from Noto, a famous old city close to Avola. High quality wines are also produced using non-native varietals like Syrah, Chardonnay and Merlot. This is a miniscule beginning in fine wine but an experiment to be watched.

The largest island in the Mediterranean, Sicily's volcanic soils and mountainous vineyards overlooking the Mediterranean explain the excellent wines produced.

X

Apulia

Like Sicily, very good but not great wines are produced in Apulia. The region is probably the source of the Zinfandel grown throughout ~~northern~~ California. In Apulia the grape is called Primitivo. And the ampelographers argue that it is very slightly different than Zinfandel. But it's an intense black red with peppery characters on the palate. It ages and gets much better. In my not always humble opinion Primitivo is Zinfandel.

Apulia (Italian: *Puglia*) borders the Adriatic Sea on the east, the Ionian Sea to the southeast and the Strait of Òtranto and

Gulf of Taranto in the south. Its southernmost portion, known as Salento peninsula, forms a high heel on the "boot" of Italy.

In past decades Apulia was composed of many cooperatives which existed thanks to financial support from the Italian government. As government support was removed, the growers were forced to concentrate on quality not quantity. The consumer has been the beneficiary. The region now has 4 DOCGs and 29 DOCs, more than any other region in the south, and also six IGTs that produce increasing quantities of quality wines that are acknowledged internationally for representing good value.

Like Sicily, the mountain vineyards and the cooling of the Adriatic Sea contribute to grape farming. The region comprises 7,469 square miles and its population is about 4.1 million.

Look for Primitivo on the label. You will be buying Italian Zinfandel at a very good price.

XI

Abruzzo

The most notable wine of the region is Montepulciano d'Abruzzo produced by the Montepulciano grape that is distinct from the Sangiovese grape behind the Tuscan wine Vino Nobile di Montepulciano. The Montepulciano d'Abruzzo is best drunk young. Like Beaujolais the wine is fresh and giving when young but gets dull in old age—even just five years old.

Some Trebbiano is produced but one should not think of quality. It's cheap and mostly produced by cooperatives to be sold under private label by supermarkets. It's wine to be sure but not the stuff that dreams are made of.

Abruzzo is located in the mountainous central Italian region of Abruzzo along the Adriatic Sea. It is bordered by the Molise wine region to the south, Marche to the north and Lazio to the west. .

Today more than 42 million cases of wine are produced annually in Abruzzo, making it the fifth most productive region in Italy, but only 21.5% of which is made under the DOC) designation. The majority of the region's wine (more than two-thirds) is produced by co-operatives or sold in bulk to *negociants* in other Italian wine regions in Tuscany, Piedmont and the Veneto for blending.

While wine is produced in all four of Abruzzo's provinces, the bulk of the production takes place in the province of Chieti which is the fifth largest producing province in all of Italy. Some of the most highly rated wine from Abruzzo comes from the hillside vineyards in the northern provinces of Pescara and Teramo. In the completely mountainous province of L'Aquila in the west some Rosé wine known as Cerasuolo from the Montepulciano grape is produced. It is highly unlikely that an American or Brit will find this Rosé to purchase.

XII

Friuli/Venezia Giulia

Friuli-Venezia Giulia wine (or simply Friuli) is wine made in the northeast of Italy. Once part of the Venetian Republic and with sections under the influence of the Austro-Hungarian Empire for some time, the wines of the region have noticeable Slavic and Germanic influences. There are eleven *DOCs* and three DOCGs in the Friuli-Venezia Giulia area. The region has three IGT designations Alto Livenza, delle Venezie and Venezia Giulia. Nearly 62% of the wine produced in the region falls under a DOC designation. The area is known predominantly for its white wines which are considered some of the best examples of Italian wine. Along with the Veneto and Trentino-Alto Adige/Südtirol, the Friuli-Venezia Giulia forms the Tre Venezie wine region which ranks with Tuscany and Piedmont as Italy's world class wine regions. Available everywhere this region is the great fountain that spouts Pinot Grigio to the world.

XIII

Liguria

Liguria is small and the wines have not attracted much attention although there is investment going on. Probably, the best

Ligurian blackberry character grape is Rossese whose origins date back to at least the Fifteenth Century but other than that remain fairly obscure. The white grapes are Vermentino and Pigato.

Liguria has several DOCs with the most notable being the Cinque Terre DOC from cliff-side vineyards situated among the five fishing villages of Cinque Terre in the province of La Spezia. In the west it is the red wine producing region of Dolceacqua producing wine from the Rossese grape.

Liguria is located along the Italian Riviera and the principal city is Genoa. Lucca is where olive oil from throughout the Mediterranean is blended. Liguria is bordered by the Piedmont wine region to the north, the Alps and French wine region of Provence to the west, the Apennine Mountains and the Emilia Romagna wine region to the east with a small border shared with Tuscany in the southeast along the Ligurian sea.

XIV

Lombardy

Lombardy wine is produced in the north central Italy. The region is known particularly for its sparkling wines made in the Franciacorta and Oltrepò Pavese areas. Lombardy also produces still red, white and rosé wines made from a variety of local and international grapes including Nebbiolo wines in the Valtellina region, Trebbiano di Lugana white wines produced with the Chiaretto style Rosé along the shores of Lake Garda. The wine region currently has fifteen DOCs, three DOCGs and thirteen IGTs designations. The main cities of the region are Milan, Bergamo and Brescia. The region annually produces over 28 million gallons of wine, more than the regions of Friuli-Venezia Giulia, Marche, Trentino-Alto Adige/Südtirol and Umbria.

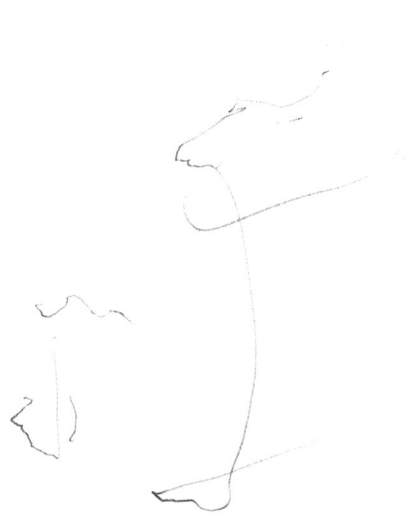

XV

Emilia – Romagna

An American company—Banfi, founded by the Mariani family of Long Island—made a spectacular market splash with Riunite, a slightly *frizzante* and sweet wine, over the past forty years. With a small price tag and an aggressive nose full of red berries, this was an introductory red wine for millions of Americans.

"Riunite on ice, it tastes nice," was the advertising tag line on television and in print for many years. The colder the better as a good chill helps the palate avoid coarseness. The Brand once topped ten million cases per year.

Banfi moved on from Riunite and now has extensive holdings in Brunello di Montalcino as well as greater Tuscany and the Piedmont. They have proven they can be successful at both ends of the price market.

Understanding Lambrusco (not to be confused with the foxy *vitis labrusca* a varietal native to Northeastern United States and definitely not in the *vitis vinifera* family of noble grapes) wine is complicated as there are thirteen to seventeen different indigenous Lambrusco grape varieties, not clones. But don't get confused with this complexity; the wine is a simple, inexpensive pleasure not to be overburdened with enological debate.

Emilia Romagna is an administrative Region comprising the historical regions of Emilia and Romagna. Its capital is Bologna. It has an area of 8,666 square miles, and about 4.4 million inhabitants. Emilia Romagna is one of the wealthiest and most developed regions in Europe, with the third highest GDP per capita in Italy. Bologna, its capital, has one of Italy's highest quality of life indices and advanced social services. Emilia Romagna is also a cultural and tourist center, being the home of the University of Bologna, the oldest university in the world, containing Romanesque and Renaissance cities such as Modena (home of great glass and balsamic vinegar), Parma (home of great prosciutto) and Ferrara (home of great palaces), being a centre for food (home of Bolognese everything), and the Italian capital of high end automobile production (home of Ferrari, Lamborghini, Maserati, Pagani, De Tomaso and Ducati) and having popular coastal resorts such as Rimini and Riccione. Foodies go there because the food is great. The wines are fairly common but don't let that stop you.

XVI

Umbria

Perhaps the only thing you will ever learn about Umbria is that the town of Orvieto is surrounded by Trebbiano vineyards and the town has given its name to the wine. Orvieto is inexpensive and ubiquitous. On a desert island were Orvieto the only wine available you would grab it readily and think it divine. As long as it was very cold.

Umbria, in central Italy, is a region of lush rolling hills, hilltop villages and iconic, historic towns (exemplified by Orvieto and Assisi). Its annual wine production of approximately 26 million gallons is less than one third that of neighboring Tuscany, and makes it the country's fourth-smallest wine-producing region by volume. Located at the very heart of the peninsula, it is hemmed in by its neighbors Tuscany, Marche and Lazio, and is in fact the only Italian region with neither a coastline nor an international border.

As of mid-2010 only around 17% of the wines produced were of DOC level, although the quality and prominence of the region's wines are on the rise. This progression can be attributed in part to the employment of consulting oenologists, a practice common in the quality wine areas of Tuscany, Piedmont and Friuli during the 1980s and 1990s. This investment has markedly improved wine based on Sangiovese (the region's principal red variety), but many of the high-quality new wines are Cabernet Sauvignon, Merlot and Pinot Noir for the reds, or Chardonnay for the whites. An Umbrian style has evolved for Chardonnay blended with Grechetto, which is barrel fermented. As these new wines cost a fraction of the price of those from neighboring Tuscany, they attract considerable interest at home and internationally.

The climate of Umbria is similar to that of Tuscany – cold, rainy winters and dry summers with abundant sunshine. The exception to this is the area west of Perugia, where temperatures are moderated by the waters of Lake Trasimeno (the largest lake on the peninsula). The majority of the region's vineyard plantings are along terraces cut into the hillsides, which is reflected in a number of the area's DOC names (*colli* means 'hills').

Trebbiano is also referred to as Procanico in Umbria, although some believe it to be a superior clone to the Tuscan Trebbiano. Although best-known for its white wines, Umbria's two DOCGs are for red wines. The native grape Sagrantino has gained prominence in the Montefalco area, creating wines of some depth and power, so it was no surprise when Montefalco Sagrantino received DOCG classification in 1992. The second of the region's DOCG wines is Torgiano Rosso Riserva. There are eleven DOCs and six IGTs--Allerona, Bettona, Cannara, Narni, Spello and the region-wide Umbria IGT.

XVII

Marche

Cesare Mondavi. Birthdate: January 20, 1883. Birthplace: Sassoferrato, Marche, Italy. Died November 29, 1959 in Napa County. Cesare was Robert Mondavi's father. An uneducated man he laid the foundation for Peter (at the Charles Krug Winery) and Robert's success. He never conquered the English language despite almost 60 years in Minnesota and California.

Marche (pronounced Mar-kay) is a region on the eastern side of central Italy. This is an unremarkable wine growing region. However the astute reader will realize now that almost every region of Italy has been counted as a wine growing region. Little Marche wine is exported. This probably reflects an inability to compete in quality with Tuscany, Piedmont, Veneto, Sicily, etc.

Marche occupies a roughly triangular area whose longer sides are formed by the Apennine Mountains in the west and the

Adriatic Sea in the east. Emilia-Romagna and Abruzzo are its neighboring regions to the north and south respectively, and it is separated from Umbria only by the Apennines.

Marche's winemaking heritage spans thousands of years and has been influenced, among others, by the Etruscans, Romans and Lombards. The presence of these various cultures goes a long way to explaining the breadth of viticultural tradition and wine styles in the region. Marche has a number of terroirs (microclimates) that are extremely well suited to the cultivation of vines, particularly among the rolling coastal hills such as those around Ancona. Due to the influences of the Apennines, the Adriatic and the region's rivers (the Metauro, Potenza, Tronto and Nera), there are various climates at work in Marche, giving wine producers both warm and cool viticultural zones to utilize. Calcareous, clay and limestone-rich soils contribute to the distinctive terroir, and vary according to the region's distinctive topography.

Marche's vineyards cover around 60,000 acres and produce almost two million hectoliters of wine annually. The majority of this is sold as Vino di Tavola or under IGT Marche. Only 20 percent is sold under the region's 15 DOC and four DOCG titles: far from the 40 percent achieved by the wines of the nation's top-quality region Piedmont, but significantly higher than is found in Sicily and Calabria, where the DOC wines make up just 5 percent of total production.

Marche is best known as a white-wine region, although it is home to some reds of high quality too. In terms of volume, the leading white varieties here are the ubiquitous Trebbiano and Verdicchio, the grape to which Marches has been a spiritual home for more than 600 years. The finest expressions of Verdicchio are found in the DOCGs Verdicchio dei Castelli di Jesi and Verdicchio di Matelica. These green-hued, green-tinged white wines are characterized by lively acidity and subtle herbaceous undertones, and are an excellent food match for seafood. Verdicchio is a wine for students on a budget. Or as picnic wine served cold. Other widely planted white grapes include Pinot Bianco, Malvasia Toscana, and Pecorino. .

Among the red wines of Marche, the finest are generally made from Montepulciano or Sangiovese, the dark-skinned varieties that dominate central Italian reds.

XVIII

Sardinia

The island of Sardinia has long been known in wine circles as a producer of corks—but not wine. This is changing as Europe seeks out inexpensive wine. The preeminent red grape on the island is Cannonau, a clone of Grenache (Garnacha) brought from Seville in Spain. Sardinia was a Spanish island until the 13th Century.

Cannonau di Sardegna is a wood-aged powerhouse once characterized as 'Sardinian dynamite'. You might find it in the States. It's cheap and---dynamite.

XIX

Bubblies & Dessert Wines

Want to stun your friends? Give a dinner party and finish with Vin Santo. They will talk about you and the dinner for eons.

Vin Santo or Vino Santo (holy wine) is a style of Italian dessert wine. Traditional in Tuscany, these wines are often made from white grape varieties such as Trebbiano and Malvasia. The wines may also be described as straw wines since they are often produced by drying the freshly harvested grapes on straw mats in a warm and well ventilated area of the house. However several producers dry the grapes by hanging on racks indoors. While the style is believed to have originated in Tuscany, examples of Vin Santo can be found throughout Italy and is an authorized style of wine for several DOCs and IGTs.

The sweet Recioto delle Valpolicella dessert wine has been the style historically associated with the Veneto region and can trace its origins to winemaking techniques of the ancient Greeks. The name comes from the local dialect *recie* meaning ears. This refers to the extending lobes of a grape cluster that appear as "ears" at the top of the cluster. The exposed grapes on the "ears" usually receive the most direct sunlight and become the ripest grapes on the cluster. Historically these very ripe "ears" were picked separately and used to make very rich, sweet wines. Today the method for making *recioto* has evolved to include the use of whole grape clusters spread on drying mats for a period as long as two months. This desiccates the grapes and makes them sweeter yet. Grapes destined for Recioto della Valpolicella are often grown in the most ideally situated hillside vineyards. The grapes are taken to special drying rooms where they are allowed to desiccate, concentrating the sugars. The wines however do not achieve a high alcohol level because the fermentation is stopped by the winemaker to leave sweetness in the wine. Folks, this is a dessert wine and is intended to thrill all those with a sweet tooth.

There are *methode Champenoise* (where a secondary fermentation occurs in the bottle) Bubblies made in Italy. There are only a few and they are expensive.

But Asti Spumante is delightful and inexpensive. It's a sparkling white Italian wine made with the Moscato grape that is produced throughout southeastern Piedmont but the plantings are particularly focused around the towns of Asti and Alba. Since 1993 the wine has been classified as a DOCG and as of 2004 was Italy's largest producing appellation. In fact, in an average vintage more than ten times as much Asti Spumante is produced in Piedmont than the more well-known Piedmontese red wine Barolo. Made from the Moscato Bianco grape, it is sweet and low in alcohol, and often served with dessert. Unlike Champagne, Asti is not made sparkling through the use of secondary fermentation in the bottle but rather through a single tank fermentation utilizing the Charmat method. It retains its sweetness through a complex filtration process.

Another wine called Moscato d'Asti is made in the same region from the same grape, but is only slightly sparkling *(frizzante)* and tends to have even lower alcohol. Many California wineries, descendants of the early Italian immigrant winemakers, continue to make low residual sugar Moscato-based wine. The wine is just sweet enough to please any maiden aunt—and most other people too. Sutter Home and Robert Mondavi make a sweet Moscato in California. Many supermarkets in America carry Piedmontese Moscato wines of low sugar. They are inexpensive, sometimes as low as $5. Some are very sweet and others only slightly sweet. The label will not help the consumer choose. Only experimentation--buying different brands--will assist in the choosing of the sweetness level that is desired.

Prosecco is another tank produced (Charmat method) white Bubbly, a real value at $10-12. There is a huge production of

Prosecco from Friuli/Venezia Giulia and the Veneto. Made with Prosecco (another name for the same grape: glera) and refreshing, ubiquitous in America and the U.K. This Bubbly is a great Champagne substitute at one quarter the price. Use it to make Bellinis, for many years a summer refresher: three parts Prosecco and one part white peach purée. Serve cold like any Bubbly: 36-38°F.

Montalcino
2 x Brunello
1 x Rosso.
2 x Orcia (128)
1 x an other Orcia

Grive (6)
1 x Nipozanni + Nobile
1 x Classico - 1 an other?
1 x Pitiglano - 1 Stozi.
(6) 3

Bulgari (192)
3 x ATIS
3 x Jassante
3 x Sunlight
(9)

(21)

Terruzi
3 Arcidiavolo
3 Peperino
(6)
+ Magnum Arcidiavolo 20

28.50
58.50
87.00

Grive-in-Chian
1. Nobile (103)
3. Antinori - Reserve.
2 Classico
(6)

192
107
103
128
 80

610

176

Afterword

Here's a Euro denominated scorecard of the leading exporting regions in 2013 (just for the helluva it and for those who love numbers):

Veneto	€ 1.6B Pinot Grigio!
Piedmont	€ 970M Spumante!
Tuscany	€947M Chianti, Chianti
Trentino/South Tyrol	€476M Pinot Grigio!
Emilia Romagna	€388M Lambrusco!

The journey of reading this book hopefully leaves the reader with more anticipation and appreciation for the greatness of Italy's red wines. The Sangiovese, Nebbiolo, Corvina--and perhaps Aglianico and Barbera--grapes are grown by vintners aiming for the stars. The leap into non-native varietals such as Cabernet Sauvignon, Cabernet Franc, Merlot and Syrah has been a breathtaking ride the past several decades in the Chianti zone and Bolgheri. Every wine lover should get familiar with the rocket ship that is Italian quality in the 21st Century. The best reds age, are never chaptalized, develop complexity and soften over years of proper storage: a temperature of 55°F is likely close to ideal, and the bottles should be stored horizontally to keep the corks wet and therefore swollen.

Cent anni!

Printed in Germany
by Amazon Distribution
GmbH, Leipzig